Also by Gabriel Fackre

SECOND FRONTS IN METROPOLITAN MISSION

DO AND TELL: ENGAGEMENT EVANGELISM
IN THE '70s

WORD IN DEED

Theological Themes
in
Evangelism

by GABRIEL FACKRE

William B. Eerdmans Publishing Company

Library of Congress Cataloging in Publication Data

Fackre, Gabriel J
   Word in deed.

   Bibliography: p. 106
   1. Evangelistic work (Christian theology)
I. Title.
BV3793.F32   269'.2   74-30328
ISBN 0-8028-1605-3

   The author expresses appreciation to the *Andover Newton
Quarterly* for permission to reprint the chapter "Conversion,"
which appeared originally in Vol. 14, No. 3 (January 1974); and
to *Religion in Life* for material in Chapter 4 which appeared in
that journal as "An Acts Theology of Evangelism" in Vol. XLIV,
No. 1 (Spring 1975). Copyright ©1975 by Abingdon Press. The
writer is also grateful to Kay Coughlin, faculty secretary of
Andover Newton Theological School, for typing the manuscript.

Contents

Introduction

James P. Jones, wherever you are: Here is the explanation of the strange circumstances of July 13, 1974.

Fifty-four "evangelism consultants" of the United Church of Christ had just dispersed from a training event at LaForet, Colorado. A handful of them were on the Denver flight with you. When you got off the plane, one of them noticed your wallet on the seat. Church folk, of course, are supposed to do the right thing, so there was no doubt that your twelve credit cards had to go to the stewardess—but not without some hesitation and conversation: "Say, we've been talking all week about an evangelism that puts it all together. Here's a chance to "do *and* tell." So the group searched its soul and its luggage and came up with a homemade pamphlet from the congregation of one of us. In case you wondered about that "Explore With Us" pamphlet you found tucked alongside your American Express card—we wanted you to know a little about the word behind the deed.

What is happening here? Mainline churches making

tracts? Going out of the way to *say* something as well as
do something? These are fresh phenomena for denominations known for their reserve—yes, maybe loss of nerve
too—about sharing Christian convictions. But this
homely incident is an indication of some new currents
flowing in the mainstream churches. Some people have
found their voice, and are ready to tell their story.

These theological reflections on evangelism rise from
the midst of this momentum. They come from association
with people engaged in preparation for and practice of a
"word in deed" evangelism that runs from the risk-taking
engagement of Peter and John with the principalities and
powers of their day (see ch. 4) to a rudimentary gesture on
a Boeing 707. In fact, much of what is set forth in these
pages are lessons learned from and tested among the
people-of-God-in-mission, rather than derivatives of library research or academic debate. Perhaps it could be
called a populist theology and a peopled faith.

Still, we seek to avoid the pitfalls of an uncritical
populism by bringing the day-to-day experience of real
people into conversation with the biblical word and the
long reflection of the Christian community on it. The
theologian serves the church by facilitating a friendship
between the ancient lore and the people's religion. And
indeed, the heritage itself comes alive when it is brought
into living relationship to a church immersed in its mission. Hence, what is to be found in this book is theology
in motion, done with, by, and for the people of God.

A Personal Excursus

Evangelism touches the personal decisions and visions
of those people on the road. While the good news is first

and foremost a report of what God has done, is doing, and will do, it is also a tale of who we are and where we have been. Personal "testimony," as Harvey Cox has recently argued and classical evangelism always practiced, is the expression of a robust faith.[1] Theologians often neglect this, rarely giving a glimpse of the flesh-and-blood human behind the heady constructs. It is my hope that in this work on evangelism theology the theologian will be seen along with the theology.

But despite the intimacies, visceral outpourings, and much of the "autobiographical theology" of the day, the personal and experiential in Christian faith should be illustrative not substantive. "We preach not ourselves, but Christ crucified. . . ." Autobiography in evangelism does its work when it points beyond itself to the biography of God. Hence this Introduction seems to be the fitting place to give the personal context for what follows.

My ruminations in missiology began long before the present evangelism developments in the church. They took initial form during several years of ministry in the Chicago stockyards district and ten years of Pittsburgh steelworker mission. For some of us in the late 1940s and through the 1950s, evangelism meant winning the alienated working classes. Our models were the Iona Community, E.R. Wickham's Industrial Mission in Sheffield, England, and the East Harlem Protestant Parish. [2] My wife Dot and I spent summer 1948 hitchhiking through Great

---

1. Harvey Cox, *The Seduction of the Spirit* (New York: Simon and Schuster, 1973), pp. 9-19.

2. See E.R. Wickham, *Church and People in an Industrial City* (London: Lutterworth, 1957); George MacLeod, *We Shall Rebuild* (Glasgow: Iona Community Publishing Dept., n.d.); George W. Webber, *God's Colony in Man's World* (Nashville: Abingdon, 1960).

Britain under the auspices of the University of Chicago, studying the church and working classes, looking at strategies and methods for that mission. Our evangelism mentors were found in the World Council of Churches—and practitioner-theoreticians like Robert Spike and Don Benedict.[3] Out of this matrix came a Chicago settlement house-church ministry at 31st and Halsted, a storefront church in Homestead, Pennsylvania, a two-point charge team ministry to steelworkers, a seventy-five acre work-and-worship Milliron Community for workers and their families in the hills outside Pittsburgh.[4] Those were exciting times, and encouraging ones, as the Homestead-Duquesne parish grew over the decade from a handful to seven hundred souls.

The secular 1960s brought a shift in accent from church-oriented to world-oriented mission. My own consciousness was raised in two areas: (1) in seeing the need for extra-parochial forms of church life executed in the idiom of the culture, and (2) in recognizing acts of Jericho road compassion and justice as integral to mission. These took shape in the founding of Encounter, a coffeehouse renewal center in Lancaster, Pennsylvania, where I had gone from the parish to teach in a seminary. And they found expression in a network of freedom schools in which Dot gave leadership, a drive to integrate the city's junior high schools, the founding of a citizens' news-

3. See Amsterdam Assembly, World Council of Churches, *Man's Disorder and God's Design* (New York: Harper, 1948); Robert Spike, *In But Not Of the World* (New York: Association, 1957); Don Benedict, "Structures of the New Era," *Renewal*, III, No. 7 (Oct. 1963).

4. The Milliron community is described in *The Purpose and Work of the Ministry* (Philadelphia: Christian Education Press, 1959), pp. 114-41. In this book, and in *Under the Steeple* (Nashville: Abingdon, 1957), are to be found many of the mission themes embodied in our Chicago and Pittsburgh ministries.

paper, Dot's creative banner-making, and countless marches and demonstrations for human rights and peace in Lancaster, Washington, Mississippi, and the like during that tumultuous time.[5]

The "Missionary Structure Study" of the World Council of Churches exercised a strong pull in these latter directions, and had a significant influence on a whole generation of missioners. I was an active participant in the North American Working Group of that study, along with Jitsuo Morikawa, Hans Margull, Thomas Wieser, Colin Williams, Markus Barth, Gibson Winter, Andrew Young, Harvey Cox, Robert Spike, Letty Russell, Gerald Jud, Michael Allen, Howard Moody, Gordon Cosby, Robert Raines, George Webber, and Don Benedict. However, I was something of an irritant in this company, holding out with a few others for "naming the Name" as well as doing the deed in mission, and vigorously defending the local church and parish minister in the face of many assertions of their obsolescence and/or marginality.[6] I had the chance to work at the empowerment of local congrega-

5. Encounter and the theory of mission undergirding it are discussed in *The Pastor and the World* (Philadelphia: United Church Press, 1964), pp. 39-58, and in *Secular Impact* (Philadelphia: Pilgrim Press, 1968), pp. 74-89. Mission models developed in the human rights struggles and the formation of a citizens' newspaper are described in *Second Fronts in Metropolitan Mission* (Grand Rapids: Eerdmans, 1968), and in *Liberation in Middle America* (Pilgrim Press, 1971), pp. 92-115. On banner-making see Dorothy Fackre, "Banners of Hope," *A.D.* (United Church Edition, Shalom series), March 1973.

6. The two basic Missionary Structure Study documents are Thomas Wieser (ed.), *Planning for Mission* (New York: The U.S. Conference for the World Council of Churches, 1966), and Western Working Group and North American Working Group, *The Church for Others* (Geneva: WCC, 1967), with the running dialogue in a series of mimeographed papers identified as blue *Concept* and red *Concept,* published by the Department of Studies in Evangelism of the WCC. My detailed assessment of the missiology underlying the study is to be found in "The Crisis of the Congregation: A Debate," in D.B. Robertson (ed.), *Voluntary Associations* (Richmond: John Knox, 1966), pp. 275-97, and *Humiliation and Celebration* (New York: Sheed and Ward, 1969), pp. 68-88, 255-307.

tions for mission in the world while serving as chairman of a committee responsible for a two-year emphasis in the United Church of Christ on "The Local Church in God's Mission."

Evangelism in the 1970s has been—for Dot and me and many others—a time both of new learnings and of a quest for the wholeness of mission. The spiritual hunger in the world and the readiness of an increasing number in the churches to share the food they have are some of the new awarenesses in the seeking 1970s. We have moved from the more bashful *disciplina arcani* conception of the Word to a bolder telling of the story to James P. Jones. But there is a "get-it-all-together" commitment which goes along with that. It entails a determination to do the deed of mercy and justice as well as to speak the word (a lesson of the 1960s), and to affirm the church as well as the soul (a lesson of the 1950s).[7]

The hunger came home to me during a 1970 interlude in Hawaii while serving as theologian-in-residence at the Church of the Crossroads and teaching at the University of Hawaii. Giving sanctuary to the devotees of Hare Krishna, coming into contact with every shade of neo-mysticism on the university campus, and seeing close at hand the rise of the Jesus people movement on the islands, made me acutely conscious of a new generation starved for "meaning." Having four teen-agers, each on her own religious pilgrimage, further strengthened the belief that it was time for more solid nurture within the church and the sharing of our crust of bread with those outside the church. The preparation of a "catechism for Skye," for one of those teen-agers about to be confirmed,

7. For a discussion of this partnership see *Do and Tell* (Grand Rapids: Eerdmans, 1973), pp. 17-29, 94-106.

by our whole family, crystalized the commitment to *getting* the story.[8] Later, the response to an attempt to tell the Christian tale in the imagery of light, by way of a tract made at a summer evangelism conference and subsequently in a cassette and film, has convinced me that there is a significant audience for those ready to get the story *out*.[9]

When the United Church Board for Homeland Ministries asked me in 1972 to serve as a theological consultant to their developing evangelism thrust—one that would respond to the religious quest of the day but refuse to retreat into the popular inward-looking, world-denying piety—they found someone whose own spiritual pilgrimage had reached just that place of convergence. In the next two years, sometimes in conjunction with research and teaching at Andover-Newton and sometimes in between classes and commitments there, I worked in training programs with hundreds of evangelism enablers and consultants, and with thousands of clergy and laity at church conferences that sought to highlight the faith issues and evangelism questions. Happily, the holistic view of evangelism has been gaining ground all across the denominational spectrum, and my circuit-riding has brought me into colleagueship with kindred spirits from a wide variety of Christian communions.[10]

8. "A Catechism for Today's Storytellers," *Youth*, XXIII, No. 7 (July 1972), 23-42; *Do and Tell*, pp. 30-45.

9. *Evangelism for a New Day*, I, No. 4 (July 1973), 2; "A Tale of Light," cassette produced by Tidings, Nashville, 1974; "Getting the Story Straight," film produced by the United Church Board of Homeland Ministries, New York, 1974.

10. Closest ecumenical contact has been with the United Methodist Church leadership engaged in developing the "New Life Mission." See *New Life Mission Handbook* (Nashville: Tidings, 1974).

The mission trajectory has carried through all these years and reaches now into this small study. Here the themes developed in the recent past of popular interpretation are deepened. In particular, the theological assumptions implicit in the companion work, *Do and Tell,* are rendered explicit.

The determination to do theological work that will help equip the church for its mission thrusts me beyond the present inquiry toward a more detailed effort to state the fundamentals of Christian faith. The decades in mission and apologetics propel this missionary and apologist toward a systematic theology. I hope to devote my next sabbatical year to launching that long-range project.

I confess to a certain sadness in chronicling current commitments and future aspirations. There are very few in the theological guild who seem to share either of these interests or inclinations—providing theological resources for the evangelism movement in the churches, or working at a fresh, systematic articulation of Christian faith. For me the two are intimately related: as you struggle to get the story out, you are driven back to getting the story straight. I have a hunch that these passions of mine rise from my deep immersion in the life of the church, and the belief that theology is done best in the context of the church, as that church is in mission in the world. I covet for my brothers and sisters researching and writing in theology this same kind of work along the missionary edges of the church. The sought-for theological renaissance will take place to the extent that we have that kind of participatory and populist reflection. In fact, the lively theology of today is found among Latin American theologians concentrating in just these two areas mentioned, such as Orlando Costas' skillful and intriguing work in the theology of evangelism and Gustavo Gutierrez's rejuvenation of constructive theology.[11]

A final testimony. While this brief journey discloses something of the concrete "I" behind the intellectual abstractions, the record might just as well have read "we." Not an editorial "we," but a conjugal one, a partnership in mission in which husband and wife have worked and thought, played and prayed together, every step of the way.

Subject Matter

As reflection that has happened "on the road," according to the issues that have emerged in the preparation and practice of evangelism, this short study is no attempt at systematic missiology. It is not a theology of evangelism but evangelism/theology, the encounter of the discipline of theology with the day-to-day evangelism struggle and its attendant questions: what is it? how do we do it faithfully? what can we expect from it? The answers to those questions have been tested and refined time and again in the field among those aggressively engaged in mission.

Our treatment of the cultural context of evangelism is brief, since *Do and Tell* gave more detailed attention to the neo-mystical and neo-pietist developments in our society, and the evolution of interest in evangelism in the churches over the past few years.[12] But in the first chapter ("Orientation") there is a reworking and updating of the

11. Orlando E. Costas, *The Church and its Mission: A Shattering Critique from the Third World* (Wheaton: Tyndale, 1974); Gustavo Gutierrez, *A Theology of Liberation* (tr. and ed. Sr. Caridad Inda and John Eagleson) (Maryknoll, New York: Orbis, 1973).

12. *Do and Tell*, pp. 9-29, 79-93.

analyses in *Do and Tell*. In the same chapter, which seeks
to get the reference points clear, we examine the question
of definition, both a broader meaning and then a nar-
rower, working definition for the kind of ''Acts
evangelism'' assumed throughout the study.

Just what *is* the good news we have to share? What is
the story we have ''to tell to the nations''? In average
church circles, too long inattentive to their own basic
faith, this has become a priority in the preparation for
evangelism. In the training and consciousness-raising I
have engaged in over the past three years, I have developed a way of ''getting the story straight'' that appears
in the chapter on proclamation. Of course, *the* story
comes out as *our* story, in that it is not a God's-eye view of
the redemptive events, but a perception from our finite
angle of vision, reported in imagery that one storyteller
finds apt for this time and place. The hope is that it will
evoke from others a reading of the deeds of God that
comes out of symbols and settings meaningful in theirs.

In countless discussions about the nature of the Christian faith the questions recurs: what is your authority for
what you say about evangelism and the evangel? How do
you get *to* the story? In the chapter on authorization, the
interrelations of Scripture, tradition, and experience are
examined, using figures that are consistent with the
theme of story: the storybook, the storytellers, and storyland.

How do you get the story *out* once you get to it and get
it straight? The action chapter deals with some key pas-
sages from the Book of Acts, which describe the
evangelism of the first evangelists. The rise of evangelism
in mainline churches brings with it the rediscovery of the
Bible, and this exciting reappropriation of the storybook

has opened up fresh vistas. The exegesis of Acts 3 and 4, and its translation into contemporary terms, is one of the results.

What happens when the good news goes out effectively, when healthy seed falls on fertile soil? Getting the story *in* is the result of getting it out. The chapter on conversion is an examination of the change of direction in persons that issues from authentic evangelism.

Themes and Commitments

There are some refrains throughout this study. One of them is a reach for the fulness of the gospel and the wholeness of approach: reductionism is resisted in the definition of evangelism; the witness of Scripture, tradition, and experience is affirmed, although priorities are also established; in the articulation of the Christian saga no chapter is censored; in the analysis of apostolic mission the many-facetedness of the evangelism process is stressed; and in the examination of conversion, all the "turning points" that constitute the full about-face are honored.

A special effort at wholeness is made in relation to the word and deed ingredients of Acts evangelism. In fact, the uniqueness of the movement of evangelism of which the theology in this book is a megaphone is precisely a commitment to this union.

The occupational hazard of an earlier period of mission which stressed the importance of changing institutions was the tendency to ignore the individual. One of the crucial contributions of evangelism to the larger mission of the church is its focus on the self, its address to the decisional center of a person, and its attention to the birth of a new being. Sister Mary Irma's sensitive declaration at

the bedside of a dying patient expresses this kind of care
for "the single one" (Kierkegaard) integral to evangelism.

NO SPARROW FALLS

I am weary of universals.
I would see for an hour only small, individual
    things—
Gray velvet wings
Of one moth toward one white candle;
Not Life, but one moth flying;
Not Death, but one thing dying;
Not Light, but one pale yellow flame draining from
    one white taper;
Not Time, but the third hour of one autumn night.
Not Man, but a man is born, and at one hour;
And at one hour he dies.
And as I kneel here by the particular bed that
    supports the dying body,
I commend a soul, one, indivisible, immortal,
To the God who has numbered the hairs of the head
And marks the fall of the sparrow.[13]

A single one, however, is not a solitary one, an insight
that eluded Kierkegaard and is neglected by much conventional evangelism. No human being is an island.
Everyone is part of the mainland of social, economic, and
political structures. Because this is so, evangelism needs
other aspects of mission as its allies, including those
whose priorities are the institutions and systems that envi-
ron each decision-maker. More than that, the evangelist
as evangelist cannot avoid dealing with principalities and
powers as well as persons, as Peter and John found out

13. In John G. Brunini (ed.), *Sealed Unto the Day* (New York:
Catholic Poetry Society of America, 1955), p. 47.

when they confronted the power structure of their day. And the evangelist as evangelist is a true agent of the Spirit's work of conversion only when the turned person has turned toward the neighbor in need of humanization within and from the systems and structures that dehumanize.

The Bible has been mentioned as the theater in which the drama of evangelism develops. The book of the story is foundational to all that is said here. It is the charter of evangelism, and its rediscovery underlies this exposition of mission. Learning from the apostles about evangelism, of course, is more than mechanically repeating what the first evangelists did and said. The Holy Spirit has been moving in the church and the world for two thousand years, teaching us fresh ways in new times to carry out the mission they launched. We must, therefore, listen for the special word that comes to us through the words of the apostles, a word that will guide us in our time and our way to do what they did in theirs.

A companion commitment is the reappropriation of the ancient code-words of the Christian faith. Gospel, salvation, conversion, new birth, repentance, even evangelism—these terms are not the exclusive property of one strand of Christianity. This language belongs to the whole Christian community. And when the whole community begins to repossess these terms their meaning will begin to reflect that catholicity, growing away from parochialism into the fuller and richer texture of their origins.

A commitment to communicate is also basic to what follows. If evangelism is getting the story out, the medium must somehow facilitate the message. The idiom, consequently, cannot be arcane. If we want people to understand, then the code language of the faith community must be translated into terms meaningful to our contemporaries. I have tried to do this without vulgarizing or using the jargon of popular culture, but by appropriating figures that have both a history in Christian tradition and contemporaneity in our culture. Thus the figures of light and storytelling play an important role. This is not "mythological," in the sense of salutary fiction. It is the use of sounds and sights from our day-to-day world to steward the mysteries of God. Obviously this metaphorical theology is not directly exportable from earth to heaven. It is our portion now only to "see through a glass darkly." But the God made known in the flesh and blood of Jesus Christ is best proclaimed in flesh-and-blood terms to flesh-and-blood people.

And this book is for flesh-and-blood people. We end where we began, with the people of God. This small work will have served its purpose if real evangelists, clergy and lay, working along the front line of mission, discover it to be of some use. It is for those who want to find James P. Jones, wherever he is.

The Door of the Future

We may conclude this Introduction with some speculation as to where James P. Jones might be, using a metaphor to suggest the location.

Consider our era as a long, dark corridor down which proceed its people toward the door at the end, the door of the future.

One group of contemporaries edges up timidly to the threshold and perceives the door to be shut. They believe the future is closed. So they turn about and retreat back down the hallway. These are the folk who have with-drawn into nostalgia. They return to the past because the future is full of foreboding. This is the particular tempta-tion of the middle American, of Archie Bunker singing, "Those Were the Days. . . ."

Another group rushes headlong toward the end of the corridor. Or so they did in the 1960s, when visionaries believed that the door of the future was flung wide open. They thought the world could be changed by flower power or instant revolution. But when they reached the threshold, they crashed against the resisting wood. Many of them now sit stunned and passive before the door "seeing stars." Believing that the future cannot be pen-etrated, they comfort themselves with inner visions of the light behind the dark door, with astrological charts, chemical mind manipulation, or meditative neo-mysticisms.

Despair enervates. It sends the middle American into nostalgia. It immobilizes the counter-culture.

But hope mobilizes. There is a third company that makes its way down the darkened hall. What does it see? A slit of light shows along the edges of the aperture. This group perceives the door to be ajar. There *is* light at the end of the corridor. The future is open. Not wide open, for the heavy oak of evil still stands across the path. But it is not locked or shut.

Why? Someone has passed this way before. Jesus Christ has met tomorrow's barrier. On Easter morning he tore down the no exit sign and shouldered open the door to the future.

Because those in this evangelical company can see the Light, they thrust forward. They act toward the future. Christian hope liberates from the false perceptions that

drive us back, or send us in and down. Hope faces us out
and ahead, and propels us across the threshold. In times
of wandering and disspiritedness, the evangelist offers a
word in deed that beckons people to move in hope "out
of darkness . . . into marvelous light."

CHAPTER ONE

Orientation

Why Evangelism Today?

The shelves of shopping mall bookstores bulge with the revelations of the latest guru and swami. Television features the popular series "Religion in America." Long lines form at theaters showing the latest film on sorcery, exorcism, or the supernatural. Why all this fascination with religion?

Many are drawn to cult and occult because they see science and sobriety as having failed them. A world that believed in laboratories and factories, pragmatism and politics, appears to have produced ecological disaster, energy crises, poverty, inflation, wars, and Watergates. "If we can't trust the cold machinations of the West, then we'll try the warm mysteries of the East"—so it is said.

Behind the thirst for mystery is the quest for meaning. Decades of scientism and secularity had silenced gnawing questions like the one put in the mouth of Judas in *Jesus Christ Superstar:* "I only want to know. . . ." I want to *know* about life and death, divine reality and human destiny, the stubbornness of evil and the possibilities of hope. The answer of the secular city, "No comment," is no longer good enough.

To those who hunger for mystery and meaning there comes a response from the church—"We've a story to tell. . . ." There is some *good news* about life, death, and destiny. There is food for those starved for hope. It is not as exotically packaged and artfully merchandised as the sweetmeats of a faddish neo-mysticism, but it is solid nourishment. As D. T. Niles put it, "Evangelism is one beggar telling another beggar where to find bread."

Some other things are shaping the church's fresh determination to get the story out. The discontents of the day show that people are restless with old habits and dead-end directions. Weariness with wickedness in high places —and low places—makes us say, "It's time for a change." We need new visions and new decisions, yes, new beings, new persons. After an era of people who were "turned on," we need people who are "turned around." We shall explore the New Testament turning words, *metanoia* and *epistrophe,* in the chapter on conversion. Converts are those who have done an about-face, assumed a new posture, and launched a new pilgrimage. They have turned from darkness to light, from the idols of mammon and power, from the gods of arrogance or apathy, pride or lust, to the God of mercy and justice who shines in the face of Jesus Christ. And the turned ones are those who not only see the Light, but who see *in* the Light the wretched of the earth, and seeing, serve the neighbor in need.

To crave change, to hope for changed lives and a changed nation, is to be open to the promise that the story we have to tell will turn people around. Evangelism is the

response the church is making to the anguished awareness that it is time for a new direction.

Dissatisfaction with the state of the church as well as
the state of the world contributes to the evangelism imperative. Discontent with the church is nothing new; we
have just been through a period of drastic self-criticism.
But now it has to do with basic survival questions. The
membership of churches generally thought to constitute
mainstream Christianity has plummeted sharply. How
many more losses can the churches sustain before they
disappear from one community after another?

Evangelism for many is the rising consciousness of this
state of affairs and a growing will to do something about
it. Evangelism in this area seeks new growth for the
church as well as new direction of life.

Why evangelism today? It is a response to a hunger for
faith, a need for change, and a concern for the future of
the church.

But the needs and hopes we have been describing are
merely the outward signs of an "inward and spiritual
grace." The human response to the needs of the hour is
made possible by the fearful and wonderful working of
the Holy Spirit. That lively Presence is at the bottom of the
restlessness in the world and the stirrings in the church. As
the evangelism thrust of the early church was empowered
by the Spirit descending on the apostles at Pentecost, so
today the winds and fires of that same Spirit are moving in
our midst.[1]

1. For an expansion of some of these themes see Gabriel Fackre,
"Evangelism: Meaning, Context, Mandate," *Christian Ministry*, IV, No.
2 (March 1973), 7-14; *Do and Tell*, pp. 9-29, 79-93; and the Introduction to *Evangelism Training Manual* (New York: United Church Board
for Homeland Ministries, 1974), mimeograph. The latter is an excellent
six-session training program for local church lay evangelists developed
by the UCBHM New Materials Task Force.

What is Evangelism?

There are almost as many definitions of evangelism as there are evangelists.[2] Evangelism is many-faceted, and we can see its richness and variety when we look at the activity of the first evangelists. But it is also important to understand the singularity of evangelism, the thing that distinguishes it from other aspects of the church's life.

A clue comes from the root of the word itself—*evangel* or good news. To the first Christians who used the term it meant the announcement of divine action to bring humanity, nature, and God together. It is the story of the deeds of God from creation to consummation, with the highlight on its central chapters: Bethlehem, Galilee, Calvary, and Easter—Jesus Christ. Evangelism is getting that story out.

The word "out" is critical. Evangelism is one aspect of the church's outward-thrusting mission. Its focus is the outsider not the insider. It is not synonymous with the renewal of the church, growth in the Christian life, or the nurture of the Christian community, although this "in-reach" is preparatory to and the environment of evangelism outreach.[3]

But that tale is no conventional chronicle. It is not a report that can be turned off casually like the evening news. It upsets, exhilarates, wounds, heals, liberates, reconciles. It changes things! It converts. It turns people around.

Evangelism, therefore, in a broad sense that includes a

2. For example see the compilation found in "Perspectives on Evangelism," *JSAC Grapevine*, V, No. 2 (July 1973).

3. The relation of inreach to outreach is discussed in *Do and Tell*, pp. 97-99.

variety of practices is getting out the story that turns people around. Wherever that kind of event is taking place, evangelism is happening.

From the perspective of the theology in this book not all that goes under the label "evangelism" is a full and faithful embodiment of biblical witness. Contemporary evangelism is plagued by reductionist conceptions which can seriously hamper the task of getting the story out. While God can and does use even our fragmented vessels for the divine treasure, we live under the mandate of the wholeness of evangelism set forth in the New Testament. And we shall give concentrated attention to that full rhythm found in the evangelism of the first evangelists.

Anticipating the analysis of apostolic evangelism in the Book of Acts, we refine the broad definition: *Acts evangelism, or action evangelism, is empowerment by the Holy Spirit to get the story out, by word in deed, so that people will be turned around to Jesus Christ, into his body the church, and toward the neighbor in need.* Or, in the New Testament imagery to which we shall allude throughout, evangelism is the declaration of the wonderful deeds of God who brings us out of darkness into marvelous light, and in that light enables us to see the wretched of the earth and the brother and sister in Christ.

Just what is this story we are called to get out? How can we recount it in terms meaningful to our time and place? We turn to the exposition of the kerygma, the proclamation.

CHAPTER TWO

Proclamation

The Massachusetts Conference of the United Church of Christ had been through some deep involvements recently—a million-dollar grant for black development, a strong stand on prison reform, aggressive support for Cesar Chavez, a Paris peace witness by its leader Avery Post. Together with many others, the activist UCC constituency was beginning to feel some new kinds of stirring in the early 1970s. Denominational jargon soon found the label for it: "the faith priority."

To understand what the faith priority might mean for our part of the world, the Massachusetts Conference leader and I, pastor and teacher, began making the rounds to hear from and speak to the people—about the fundamentals. After singing a hymn long discarded (but with surprisingly fresh imagery), "We've a Story to Tell to the Nations," Avery Post would put the question, "What *is* the story?" What are the basic perceptions of life and death, God and humanity, Christ and salvation, which make us who we are and plunge us, heirs of New England Congregationalism, into the agonies of the civil community? What drove our ancestors out the door of Old South Church two hundred years ago to dump British tea into Boston harbor? What is it that brings us regularly to this quaint building on the village green to sing strange songs and engage in esoteric practices? What is this vision, this hope, this faith that gives us our basic identity?

One of the lessons learned from these visitations was that before you can get the story *out* you have to get it *straight*. Excited evangelistic calls that do not take into account the condition of faith in congregations either fall on deaf ears or degenerate into public relations ventures.

What getting the story straight entails was brought home to us by a simple exercise in theologizing. Small groups gathered to ponder Mr. Post's question. In the reporting and discussion that followed we became very aware of a keen interest on the part of the churches in the quest for depth and clarity of faith. Furthermore, there is a good deal of profound grappling and searching religious judgment in local congregations (which are frequently disdained by the critics of institutional religion). Especially apparent in our dialogues was the experiential character of the affirmations and observations made. As in the wider society now actively exploring the feeling dimension of selfhood, so, too, in the church the personal is to the foreground. This interiority is a genuine plus.

But if the process of getting it *in* is making headway, the job of getting it *straight* is having a rougher road. The danger of the intense personalization of faith is the transformation of the good news into a report of where we have been and what we have felt, rather than what God has done, is doing, and will do. Or it may make for so selective a reading of the Christian story that the tale looks more like my autobiography than the biography of God.

Thus, one of the crucial tasks of the church today is the development of the capacity to feel *my* story and tell *our* story. And the story we have to tell has to be the whole one, not an abridgment made according to each one's private agenda and range of perception. Getting all the chapters together—getting it straight—is a necessary companion of getting it in, and a condition of getting it out.

The new interiority suggests another ground rule for communicating the Christian faith today. Times in search of the visceral and elemental cry out for a flesh-and-blood theology. People at the grassroots of church life themselves have great gifts of imagery and respond to a faith exploration that honors that sensibility. Storytelling that connects, therefore, will be (in Sallie Teselle's terms) "metaphorical theology."[1] Getting it *down* to concretion, therefore, is a partner challenge to getting it straight.

Out of this running conversation with people in the churches have emerged some clues to communication. One of them is an extended metaphor that captures the salient happenings in the Christian drama, using the imagery of light. It is the kind of attempt at storytelling in communicative idiom that I am convinced we must be about today, both within and beyond the faith community.

Light

The film about Saint Francis, *Brother Sun, Sister Moon,* drew an audience in Boston that ran from the blue-jeaned to the blue-collared. While the attraction of this some-

1. Sallie Teselle, "A Trial Run: Parable, Poem, An Autobiographical Story," *Andover Newton Quarterly,* XIII, No. 4 (March 1973), 277-87.

what trivialized portrayal of Franciscan flight to the communal and natural may have been related to countercultural protest, its broad appeal also had something to do with the controlling imagery of light. Today's fascination with light runs from the rainbow commune and sunburst shawl of the counterculture to the Bright Star Motel and sun-kissed orange juices of middle America. These contemporary flashings go deep into the memory of the race, perhaps even into its archetypal origins. Light is still a potent symbol in the 1970s.

As light figures pervade our contemporary culture, so they also suffuse the pages of the Bible. "There is hardly another pair of metaphors so often used in both the Old and the New Testaments as 'groping (or stumbling) in the dark' and 'walking in the light.' "[2] In the Old Testament: "The Lord is my light and my salvation; whom shall I fear" (Ps. 27:1 NEB); "In thy light we are bathed with light" (Ps. 36:9 NEB); "The Lord make his face shine upon you and be gracious to you" (Num. 6:25 NEB); "Fools who long for the day of the Lord, what will the day of the Lord mean to you? It will be darkness, not light" (Amos 5:18 NEB); "I will make you a light to the nations, to be a salvation to earth's farthest bounds" (Isa. 49:6 NEB); "The people who walked in darkness have seen a great light; the light has dawned upon them, dwellers in a land as dark as death" (Isa. 9:2 NEB). In the New Testa-

2. Bela Vassady, *Light Against Darkness* (Philadelphia: Christian Education Press, 1961), p. 12. This book is an extended commentary on the "light-overcoming-darkness" motif. In a similar vein is Edgar P. Dickie's *God is Light* (London: Hodder and Stoughton, 1953). The most detailed and searching use of this motif in contemporary theology is to be found in Karl Barth's interpretation of the prophetic office of Christ, *Church Dogmatics*, VI, 3, tr. G.W. Bromiley (Edinburgh: T. and T. Clark, 1960), passim.

ment: "All that came to be was alive with his life, and that life was the light of men. The light shines in the darkness and the darkness has not mastered it" (John 1:4-5 NEB); "I am the light of the world" (John 8:12 NEB); "You are the light for all the world. . .you, like the lamp, must shed light among your fellows . . ." (Matt. 5:15, 16 NEB); "I was on the road and nearing Damascus, when suddenly about midday a great light flashed from the sky all around me. . . " (Acts 22:6 NEB); "Let us therefore throw off the deeds of darkness and put on our armor as soldiers of light" (Rom. 13:12 NEB); "But you are a chosen race, a royal priesthood, a dedicated nation, and a people claimed by God for his own, to proclaim the triumph of him who has called you out of darkness into his marvelous light" (I Pet. 2:9 NEB); "God is light, and in him there is no darkness at all" (I John 1:5 NEB).

The biblical light refrains are repeated in Christian tradition. Commenting on the World Council of Churches' 1961 Assembly theme, "Christ, the Light of the World," Jaroslav Pelikan observed that "it selected an image that has played a major role in the history of . . . Christian theology."[3] In his fine work on the theme of light, Pelikan goes on to explore its formative role in patristic thought, especially Athanasius, and its Eastern Orthodox heirs.

A quick way into the light metaphors of Christian tradition is by way of a hymnal, where a casual survey will not only turn up numerous hymns with light as the dominant theme ("Joyful Joyful We Adore Thee," "O Splendor of God's Glory Bright," "Lead Kindly Light," "The Morning

---

3. Jaroslav Pelikan, *The Light of the World* (New York: Harper, 1960), p. 14.

Light is Breaking," "Christian Dost Thou See Them"), but also the use of light imagery in countless others. One of the earliest known Christian hymns celebrates the

> Serene Light of the Holy Glory
> Of the Father Everlasting
> Jesus Christ.[4]

Can the power of light symbolism be harnessed to contemporary storytelling? I think so. But there are several cautions.

One of them regularly confronted classical Christian thought, as theologians of light sought to distinguish their use of this symbolism from the nature religions and mysticisms that also made prolific use of this imagery. The phenomena of light do not in themselves disclose ultimate truth. One cannot find out the ultimate nature of things by looking at rainbows, sun, moon, or stars. The course of the sun does not, in and of itself, describe the arc of cosmic and human life. Christian storytelling gets its fundamental clues from events in history, not from the cycles of nature. However, as Augustine found traces of the Trinity in nature because the God of the cosmos is the same God at work in history, we too can appropriate nature symbols to interpret faith. But they must be used as servants, not masters of truth, refined and reordered by a Light that comes from a source deeper than the rhythms and beauties of natural light.

Also, before we use this symbolism, we must face a more contemporary hesitation—the association of the color black with evil in the racist undercurrents of Western thought. Does the imagery of light and darkness fall under the same censure? Black students and friends have

4. *Ibid.*, p. 31.

opened my eyes to the following: (1) Light is not in any sense of the word the property of white persons. Light is made up of the whole spectrum of color. The phenomenon of "black light" is an indication of the range of this figure. To assume that light equals white is yet another example of the assumption of Caucasian superiority. The symbol belongs to us all. (2) Dark is not synonymous with black. Dark is not a color itself but an adjective descriptive of colors, as in dark red, dark green. And darkness is the absence of light, the counterpoint to the full spectrum of color. White racism has regularly captured the word for its own purposes, as in the disparaging term "darkies." But we are all children of darkness and children of light.

The Story

God had a dream. It was a vision of a world together. Deity and humanity were in harmony. There was serenity in nature. The storybook portrays this paradise in its opening chapters as the intent of creation. We were made for the joyful peace of Eden.

Donald Baillie describes this scene of the divine intention as a lively campfire.[5] God is the roaring blaze. Humanity is a circle of celebrative dancers, arms linked, facing each other and the light.

Can the vision be brought to be? Reality shatters the dream. Humanity loves darkness more than light. The allurements of night work their wiles, and each one in that circle turns around. An about-face breaks the arm links. Peering out into the darkness, humanity sees neither the face of the neighbor nor the glow of the fire. And a serene

5. Donald Baillie, *God Was in Christ* (New York: Scribners, 1948), pp. 205f.

nature turns ominous, as it casts back shadows of lonely dancers.

Back-turning is alienation from neighbor, nature, and God. In the language of faith the word for such estrangement is sin. The temptation to turn has its source in that dark surd of evil that occasions sin. And the wages of sin are the death of the dream.

But the dream will not down. A spark from the fire finds its way into the depths of each dancer. An inner light hints of the goal. Such is the "image of God" in us—that conscience which beckons us back to the light.

Will the divine spark turn the race around? We are no lovers of the light. Our inward-bending selves smother the tiny flame. A thin spiral of smoke is the most that is left to call us to what we were meant to be. It haunts us with a sense of our destiny, but fails to turn us around.

The longsuffering Light will not let us go. At an obscure edge of the outward-faced circle the breath of God blows on a spark and there appears a "pillar of fire." Thus God signals to a fragment of rebel humanity. In the life of this chosen people, the dream is displayed. Israel is led from bondage to freedom and given a taste of a land of milk and honey. To this people come the laws of the new land, the commandments of turning to God and neighbor. In their midst rises a company of visionaries, seers of a scene of light—a world of *shalom* in which the circle is reknit, where humanity is one, as swords are beaten into plowshares, where nature is whole, as wolf and lamb lie together, where each human dwelling under vine and fig tree is free and at peace with God. In pillar, law, and prophet, the dream of liberation and reconciliation beckons.

Yet the chosen ones continue to walk the way of all

flesh. They prove to be as we all are, and their prophets declare that the Day of the Lord will be darkness not light.

What will turn the race around? Sparks and pillars will not do it. We must be found first hand. What is far must draw near. Light must *be*, as well as do.

The people who lived in darkness suddenly saw a great Light. Light became flesh and dwelt in one among us. It shone in the face of Jesus Christ. We beheld its glory! Shalom is born at Bethlehem, lives in Galilee. In him hope happens. He is our liberator, our peace, the Light of the world.

When Light comes close to those in the grip of gloom, it sears our flesh. Shalom in our midst shames our shut-up ways. The coals of love burn the enemies of Light. The disarrayed dancers recoil at the incandescence. The powers and principalities of darkness brace for the battle. On a lonely hill darkness again descends on the earth. Under the assault of the armies of night, the Light is extinguished, the dream dies.

"As Sunday morning was dawning, Mary Magdalene and the other Mary went to look at the grave. . . ." The odyssey of light moves to its climax. The grave could not bury the dream nor the night restrain the dawn. In the mysterious encounter on the cross, the powers of sin and death meet their match. The conquest of the powers of darkness is heralded by the rising dawn. Night is over. It is a new Day. Easter sunrise declares the victory of the Lord of light over the enemies of night.

Yet it is not a shadowless noonday, but dawn. There are still shadows on the land. The retreating powers of darkness brood over the world—corporate structures oppress and enslave, personal whispers lure us to pride, cosmic irrationalities tempt us to despair. Sin persists and death is still our common lot. While the promise fills the horizon, the meridian awaits a yet-to-be. This is the difference between the dawning of the age of Easter and the dawning of the age of Aquarius. There is no instant sunshine in soul or society. Full sunburst is the imagery of the Aquarian, but it is the dawnburst that represents the Christian tale. Daybreak announces the demise of night, the continuing struggle with the shadowside, and the promise of a zenith when light will be "all in all."

But it *is* dawn. Even as we live in the half-light of an already/not yet, the light is reflected and refracted on earthly terrain. A Christic world shines with possibility. Portents of the sunburst-to-be, signs of shalom, can be discerned. Wherever there is liberation and reconciliation among neighbor, nature, and God, earnests of hope happen and the future breaks in.

What of the disoriented dancers? Light scorned must suffuse, penetrate, and embrace this vagrant disassembly. It radiates their horizon. Its warmth presses on their backs. Some night wanderers are drawn by the inescapable rays of daybreak. A divine power is at work that wrenches them loose from the grip of the powers of night. They make a turn and sight the sun. They see the Light.

In Christian lore, this time of turning is the movement of conversion—turning away from the darkness (repentance) and turning to the Light (belief). It is a front-turning that brings into view in the light of the dawn a hidden humanity. Dawn-seers see *by* the Light as well as see the Light.

They see the neighbor in need. Dawn gives vision to see the wretched of the earth. Their eyes are opened to the victims felled along the Jericho Roads that stretch toward the horizon. They see and serve.

Thus sun-seers are not sun-gazers. Sun-sitting is another spirituality, one that makes for immobility and blindness to the neighbor's need. Dawn pilgrims do not stare at the light but use it to illumine their journey. They make solar sightings—of such is the life of prayer and worship—but their eyes are on the road and their feet move in pilgrimage.

Dawn light brings pilgrims together. Seeing in the light is seeing the brother and sister in Christ, as well as the neighbor in need. They are not solo travelers engrossed in private ruminations; they form a family of the Way, the children of light. Thus the envisioned circle shattered by the darkness begins to reknit as a new humanity. Not yet the full-formed ring of the final day, still hobbled by half-turns and half-light, this dawn people of God form a band traveling abreast, eyes opened to see each other, to celebrate their common goal, and to serve.

Dawn people open their ranks to those wandering in other ways. "Come over here and join us. Try this direction. You can see the light." Getting out this morning news makes pilgrims bearers of an evangel, evangelists. Dawn people are dawn pointers. Their fingers point, not up and out of this world, but ahead to the horizon God, who summons on a journey in and through the world.

Dawn sighting, serving, companying, celebrating, and pointing. In these acts the Christian Tale brings us to its present chapter. It is here that God's story merges with our stories. In this time between the already and not yet, we become characters in the unfolding plot. Not just those who have made a turn. The whole human race lives, and moves, and has its being in this Light. Unaware of their Easter origins, other peoples, movements, and pieties may mirror some of the light of the new age. The evangelist points them to the source of their shalom so they may orient themselves to it. The drama develops as the *dramatis personae* use the visions they have to seize the day that is theirs.

Our small acts are taken in the embrace of that larger drama that unfolds from creation to consummation. Our pilgrimages are part of the larger odyssey of light, one in which darkness turns to dawning, and dawning to noonday bright. And in this dawn time of promise we live by the rays of a shalom that shall be, when "Christ's great Kingdom shall come to earth, the Kingdom of love and light."[6]

6. The theological theme of dawn was first suggested to me by a song, "Dawn People," written by my folk-singer daughter Bonnie.

CHAPTER THREE

Authorization

"If that is the story, where did you get it? How do we know it is a true reading? How do I avoid passing off *my* story as *the* story?" Many questions like these came in the wake of the exercise that followed Avery Post's invitation to theology.

Pursuing the story metaphor, we may call this the matter of "authorship." Where is the author, the one who will authenticate what is being said? What is the authorization for the story?

Indeed, this is the ancient question of authority. It is as old as the second-century debate between Irenaeus and the Gnostics, and Marcion's attempt to limit the scriptural canon to an edited version of Luke and ten of Paul's letters. The issue has emerged in Christian history under different labels: revelation and reason, theology and philosophy, Scripture and tradition, God's word and human words, the church and the Bible, human experience and divine truth. At the center of it is the question of the sources and norms of Christian teaching. Where do we turn to get the gospel? If we are to *get* the story, how do we *get to* the story? Evangelism theology must deal with theological method; the way into the story is intimately bound up with the story itself.

The quandary tends to appear with particular insistence in times when there is confusion about the message. It comes to the fore also when there is a particularly vigorous statement of the meaning of faith with dubious credentials. In the early centuries of Christianity a popular Gnosticism (Docetism) produced pictures of Christ whose full humanity was seriously eroded. The response of Christian thought at that time, which found expression in the church's baptismal rites, was to set forth a simple confession of faith, a version of which is still among us in the Apostles' Creed. Also, the attempt to deal with perceived deviance came in the development of a canon of authoritative writings in the light of which statements about Christ were scrutinized. Further boundaries were set by the seats of authority in churches that traced their lineage to the apostles themselves. Thus apostolic teaching, apostolic Scripture, and apostolic ministry became the standards for sound doctrine in the early quest for christological identity.[1]

Many of the same dynamics are at work today. Thus the popular premises, the conventional wisdom of our time, find their way into conceptions of Jesus abroad in the church. Surely there is merit in the attempt to interpret the meaning of Christ in the language and thought-forms of the day; indeed, this is what we tried to do in the previous chapter. Furthermore, the Holy Spirit leads us into ever new understandings of dimensions of Jesus Christ and the story, which were not fully grasped in earlier periods. But

1. For a survey of these developments see J. N. D. Kelly, *Early Christian Doctrines* (New York: Harper, 1958).

when the current world-view becomes the controlling theme in updating and translating, the chief character in the story becomes a puppet rather than a living actor and Christ becomes captive to limited perceptions and self-serving agendas. Malachi Martin has recently sketched the Jesus figure in current and past history whose clothing changed according to the interest of the writer.[2] Albert Schweitzer's New Testament research led him to conclude that the popular nineteenth-century descriptions of Jesus reminded him of a figure who looked down into a well and saw at the bottom his own reflection (G. Tyrell's image). Renan's refined lecturer-Christ, Bruce Barton's salesman-Christ, the nineteenth-century reformer - and - revolutionary Christ, all these and many more reappeared in our Massachusetts visitations.

Are there ways we can honor the genuine attempts to find Jesus as our contemporary and at the same time respect his freedom to be who he is? Can we relate the story to the times without capitulating to them? Where do we go to get that story straight?

There are three sources of the story which perennially claim attention: the Scriptures of the Old and New Testaments, the tradition of the church, past and present, and living experience, personal and corporate. To keep the descriptions consonant with our major figure of a story, let us refer to these as (1) the storybook—the Scriptures; (2) the storytellers—the church's wisdom, ancient and contemporary; and (3) storyland—our own world of private and public experience.

Storybook, storytellers, and storyland quite rightly engage the interests of those in quest of the Christian mes-

2. Malachi Martin, *Jesus Now* (New York: Dutton, 1973).

sage. For in that story the chief author and actor brings faith alive in us through the agency of the Holy Spirit. The Spirit is present in and through the biblical record of the happenings of God, pressing those events home to us. The Spirit moves also in the community of those in each generation who struggle to tell and celebrate the story. The Spirit roams the larger landscape of human history to stir up fresh understandings and accents. Thus the living word of God brings into our reach the news of God's deeds.

How do these sources of the story relate to each other, and how ought we to relate to them? It is possible to affirm the importance of each, but fail to see how they function both normatively and descriptively, that is, both as legitimate sources of the story and active givens in the way we perceive it.

One helpful device for sorting and sifting the givens and priorities is this series of concentric rings.

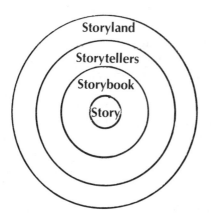

Storybook

"The Scriptures of the Old and New Testament are the ultimate rule of faith." Written into the constitutions of many denominations is this affirmation of the final standard of Christian teaching. While developed within the Protestant tradition, it is not limited to it. Cullmann has noted that Roman Catholic teaching about the primacy of the church is chronologically true, but that it was this church itself which placed above it the very biblical canon it formed.[3] Church teaching is finally accountable to the record of the eyewitnesses to the deeds of God.

The ring closest to the center is that of the storybook. The story we tell must rise from and be authenticated by the Scriptures. The authority closest to the Story, its fundamental source and norm, is the storybook, the Bible. Here are chronicled the decisive events in the saga from creation to consummation, here the epic centralities, Bethlehem, Galilee, Calvary, Easter. Here the Holy Spirit brings home the Word for us through these words about the acts of God.

There are those who choose to end the matter here. For them the Bible is the only source and norm of truth. To this methodological conviction is often conjoined the belief that at the very least God supplied the original textual autographs of the Scripture. For others it is the King James Version that is the virtual word from God's mouth. These "biblicists" draw only one circle around the story. The way in is through it alone. Church tradition is the work of humans, and human experience is the work

3. Oscar Cullmann, "Scripture and Tradition," in Daniel Callahan *et al.* (eds.), *Christianity Divided* (New York: Sheed and Ward, 1961), pp. 7-33.

of the devil. Neither can be counted as partners in the quest for Christian story. It is the business of the church and the world to listen only to the texts of the Bible.

In our exploration of authority here the Bible is honored as the "ultimate rule of faith and practice." But we reject biblicism as constricting the work of a Holy Spirit who is alive and well in the church and world, in Christian tradition and human experience. To those next rings we now turn.

Storytellers

To move beyond a one-dimensional biblicism is to learn to honor the work of the Holy Spirit in the church. God did not die and become entombed in the second century. The closing of the canon was not the lowering of a coffin lid. The living Spirit breathes in the body of Christ. Truth comes through the church's struggle to articulate the faith in and to the times in which it finds itself. The company of apostles, prophets, teachers, martyrs, and saints participates in the life of God and hence in the enlightenment God offers in this life together. The faith perceptions found in creed and council, liturgy and hymnody, preaching and teaching, theology and practice, represent that tradition in which the Spirit works and the word is to be heard. To learn from this lore is, as Karl Barth puts it, to "honor our fathers and mothers." Or, as someone else has said, "We can avoid a lot of nonsense by reading the minutes of the last meeting."

The Spirit's work in tradition takes place in the present as well as the past. The storytelling community makes its impact not only through the fathers and mothers of faith, but through the brothers and sisters as well. The mind of the church is expressed in corporate judgments as current as the Second Vatican Council or the United Church of Christ Statement of Faith. The wisdom of the contemporary church includes as well the more personal insights and visions of prophets and seers who "discern the signs of the times." These perceptions, private and public, weigh in significantly as data for story-building.

No matter how timely or laden with the pomp and circumstance of the office that announces them, the importance of ecclesiastical tradition takes second place to the authority of the Bible. We assert this in opposition to those who would take church teaching to be the weightier of the sources and norms of faith. Indeed, there is an exact counterpart to biblicism in this circle: ecclesiasticism is the belief that all there is to be known of the story can be learned from creed and council, bishop, preacher, or priest—or, in more free-flowing times, from the prophet and charismatic. Here again the assertion is made that one ring is enough. Indeed, the Spirit is at work in the Christian community from bishop to visionary, in past creed or present credo. But ecclesiasticism is to be rejected as firmly as biblicism. Church tradition must pass muster before the test of the story line. And where it also ignores the testimony of human experience, it limits its touch with the continuing narrative of the Spirit's action.

Storyland

The God of the Bible and of the church is the God of the world. The story tells of a drama in which the chief actor ranges over the heights and depths of all history and nature to accomplish the divine purposes. The worldly work of the Spirit vigorously enacts and connects the incarnate shalom within and with our own human experience. We come in touch with the Presence in the places of shalom that God is bringing to be in the world. Shalom happens in our midst whenever there is a coming together in peace and truth, liberation, and reconciliation. Where lives are freed from tyranny and injustice, where minds are liberated from ignorance and untruth, where spirits are ennobled by joy and beauty, where nature discloses its majesty and order, where estrangement is overcome by reconciliation, there is the Spirit alive and at work.

The Spirit that roams through the world as giver of truth, beauty, and goodness is the Spirit of the Triune God, and therefore, the Spirit of Jesus Christ. The signs of its presence are identifiable by the mark of the incarnate shalom.[4]

It is Christ himself who is present incognito wherever the Spirit of peace and freedom breaks through. Those in quest of the Christian story must attend to the tale that is being told in the events of human experience manifesting healing and hope. The fundamental story recorded in the storybook and interpreted by the storytellers cannot itself be understood aright unless it is read from the midst of that storyland in which the central actor of that drama, now as then, is active. *Testimonium Spiritus sancti internum*—the internal testimony of the Holy Spirit —makes present and real to us the good news.

The range of that Spirit is far beyond that spiritual "interiority" to which it is sometimes confined. It moves inside our whole time and place, expressing itself in high historical and cosmic events as well as in the depths of the soul. To risk the ascent to the heights and the descent to

4. See Edward Powers, *Signs of Shalom* (Philadelphia: United Church Press, 1973); Jack Stotts, *Shalom: The Search for a Peaceable City* (Nashville: Abingdon, 1973).

the depths is to position oneself in the environment of the Spirit. This is the context for understanding the text of the biblical word about the saga of shalom. The story is heard when it is read in the storybook, in the company of a community of storytellers, with their feet moving in pilgrimage through storyland.

We have located storyland on the outer ring of our diagram. As such, it is the encompassing habitat for the other circles. But it is also the bashful rather than the bold authorization of Christian faith. The ambiguity of this general human experience necessitated the enactment of that special set of singular happenings in our history which constitutes our story, and which created the storybook and brought the storytelling community to birth. Therefore, the perceptions of our experience are not self-sufficient clues to the nature and action of God. They must come into conversation with and under the scrutiny of Scripture and tradition. And finally their validity as expressions and extensions of the Christian gospel must be established by their faithfulness to the story line discerned in the storybook and among the storytellers.

Failure to affirm this critical companionship of experience with Scripture and tradition appears in this ring as a reductionism comparable to biblicism and ecclesiasticism. Let us call it experientialism. This is the special vulnerability of the so-called liberal churches, which are eager to make soundings in and adjustments to the latest cultural experience. When our experience is the master rather than the servant of the story, that narrative becomes an echo of the conventional wisdom, tamed by our agendas, and unable to do the critical work of calling the culture to account. The word of God is drowned out by the noises of men. But this drastic editing, and even silencing, of the news is not limited to culture Christianity. Whenever we become so mesmerized with how we feel, what we see and do, or who we are, that we no longer take our bearings from who God is, what God is doing, then experience is blinding us to the divine deeds.

The Journey

The pursuit of Christian truth is in this world always a journey, not arrival. We are on the right track when we have together Bible, church, and experience. But we cannot claim to have reached our destination. No statement of the story can lay claim to exhausting its meaning or capturing it without reservation. The articulation of it in a given time and place by the best lights of Scripture, tradition, and involvement is more than a private venture, more than just *my* story. Yet it can never be confused with a God's-eye view of the divine scenario. The story comes to us as *our* story, that tale which is revealed to us through Scripture, tradition, and human experience, but, for all that, is seen by us through our conditioned perceptions, and thus viewed "through a glass darkly."

CHAPTER FOUR

Action

Contemporary evangelism has much to learn from the first evangelists. We are afflicted today by partial perspectives that do an injustice to the full orb of apostolic practice traced out in the Book of Acts. A special kind of fragmentation is found in the prevailing verbal conception of getting the story out. The very title of the biblical charter of evangelism should alert us to this danger. It is not "Talks of the Disciples" but "Acts of the Apostles." Biblical witness is action evangelism.

The first evangelists' sortie, the initial thrust outside the Christian community to share the good news, is described in Acts 3 and 4.[1] An outline of a total evangelism move-

1. The parallels between Acts 3-4 and the first account of the church's proclamation and conversions in Acts 2 are striking. There is an active theory that the outlines of a "doublet" account can be found in chapters 2 through 5 (analyzed in *The Interpreter's Bible*, IX (New York: Abingdon-Cokesbury, 1954), 69-70. We choose the Acts 3-4 sequence of events because it is an evangelism situation like our own, in that it presupposes the existence of the church, whereas Acts 2 is a singular mighty act, the birth of the church itself. For a similar interpretation of the importance of the Acts 3-4 rhythm of evangelism, especially as it touches the relation of word to deed, see William Barclay, *Turning to God: A Study of Conversion in the Book of Acts and Today* (Grand Rapids: Baker, 1972), pp. 39-41; Douglas Webster, *What is Evangelism?* (London: The Highway Press, 1964), pp. 83-84, 147-51.

ment emerges in this sequence of events. Its rhythm is a
key to the nature of New Testament mission.

The way of apostolic evangelism described in Acts is
grounded in the earlier proclamation and action of Christ.
And the practice of that ministry is an exemplification of
the incarnation itself. After a review of those chapters in
Acts, we shall examine their rootage in the acts of Jesus
and the deeds of God.

Deed

"Peter and John were on their way up to the temple.
Now a man who had been crippled from birth used to be
carried there and laid every day by the gate of the temple
called 'Beautiful Gate,' to beg from people as they went
in. . . . Peter said, 'I have no silver or gold; but what I have
I give you: in the name of Jesus Christ of Nazareth,
walk' " (Acts 3:1-3, 6 NEB).

Apostolic evangelists begin their work outside the
gate.[2] They find themselves led by the Spirit into the
marketplace, where they are confronted with a suffering body. Dealing with physical hurts may not fit in neatly
with conceptions of evangelism whose settings are air-
conditioned auditoriums, revival tents, and street corner
testimonies (indeed, there will be time for talking as we
see the Acts evangelism drama unfolding), but the context
in which this storytelling goes on is that of worldly agony
and bodily need.

In the face of human hurt the evangelist uses the resources God gives. " 'In the name of Jesus Christ, walk.'

2. For a discussion of the location of the Beautiful Gate (Shushan or
Nicanor Gate) see *The Interpreter's Bible*, IX, 54; and S. Corbett, "Some
Observations on the Gateways to the Herodian Temple in Jerusalem,"
Palestine Exploration Quarterly, LXXXIV (1952), 7-15.

Then he grasped him by the right hand and pulled him up'' (Acts 3:7 NEB). The Spirit empowers the evangelist to do a deed of shalom in which a broken body is made whole. Apostolic evangelists are called to minister to physical needs found outside the temple. And evangelism dares a miracle of healing.

Why does apostolic evangelism begin with an act of mercy? First of all, the good news which the evangelist is called to report is the foretaste in Jesus Christ of a healed creation. The ultimate reconciliation of the world includes the knitting together of things physical as well as things spiritual. Testimony to that triumph must therefore include a witness to the promised wholeness of hope. As Emerson said in another connection, "the end pre-exists in the means." The end to which the evangelist points, the fulfilment of the vision of shalom, should appear in the act of pointing. Evangelism in this sense is "hope in action,"[3] a medium in which the message comes clear, a *deed* of the proclaimed future. The Christian story's thrust and climax, the drama of liberation and reconciliation, must pre-exist in the act of storytelling itself. The kerygma, therefore, has to be communicated in a style and setting that authenticates its hope for a world in which swords are beaten into plowshares, wolf and lamb lie down together, the blind see, the deaf hear, prisoners are visited, the hungry are fed, and the captives are liberated.

In the second place, the events that took place outside the Beautiful Gate, and many counterparts in the rest of Acts, are more than imperatives to imitate the vision of God. They are miracles of the future. That is, they are signs that the powers of night have been overcome and

3. The title of Hans Margull's study of the impact of eschatology on mission. Tr. Eugene Peters (Philadelphia: Muhlenberg, 1962).

that the horizon light is making its presence felt in the world. Because the future of God has broken into history, the unexpected can happen. Out of nothing—"I have no silver or gold" (Acts 3:6)—shalom takes form. Thus the confirmation of the evangelist's message takes place in an act of empowerment; the truth about the proclamation that the powers of night have been routed is signaled by an actual routing of those powers. And it is a victory that flies in the face of all the evidence of the evangelist's weakness and lack of resources.

Apostolic evangelism is thus grounded in both the eschatological imperative and the eschatological reality. The evangelist is called to set up a sign to the wholeness of the promised shalom and is empowered to do a deed of the future, one that boggles the mind of those who do not expect miracles, one that witnesses to the inbreaking of the Kingdom of God.

We make this passage our own today—but not by importing it in packaged fashion across the centuries. Convinced that the Holy Spirit has been at work in two millennia of the church's life and is now aggressively in our midst, we ask how that Spirit has done deeds of shalom in evangelists *since* Peter and John and works miracles of healing and hope in our time. New occasions teach new ways of performing old miracles. How that mandate is heard and how the reality of the future's presence expresses itself through us is something we must discern and do in our own way. That evangelists are called to be present in the midst of the suffering outside the gates of our temples and to think the unthinkable and do the undoable—this is the perennial substance of an action evangelism ever in quest for fresh forms.

Word

Mission moves on. In the midst of the deed comes a word: "Why are you surprised at this? . . . the God of Abraham, Isaac and Jacob, the God of our ancestors has given divine glory to . . . Jesus" (Acts 3:13 TEV). Out of Peter pours the story. We hear of the God active in Israel, incarnate in Christ, despised, suffering, and rejected. We hear of the resurrection of the one who is our shalom, the celebration of this Easter glory by witnesses, the sign of its triumph in acts of shalom, and the promise of universal restoration. Do you want to know what is afoot in this deed done? asks Peter. It is the enactment of the tale of the God who was, is, and is to be.

Getting the good news out means telling it as well as doing it. Humans have to hear a word about the inrushing future addressed to their personal center, as well as see and feel the impact of it in deeds of the Kingdom. Evangelism is a ministry of meaning. It speaks to the quandaries of life, death, and destiny. For the ancient hearer it sought to interpret the saga of God as that history intersected the hearer's own story. To the citizen of today, hungry for meaning, starved for too long by a secular, technocratic, and pragmatic world which has asked only "how" and never "why and wherefore," a world now sampling exotic Oriental menus of meaning, it offers nourishment.[4]

As with deed, so with word, the way that the story is best communicated is in the idiom of the times, forged by the Spirit living and working in those times. For the first-century apostle preaching to Israel, it will be a story

4. On the contemporary quest for meaning see Dean Kelley, *Why Conservative Churches Are Growing* (New York: Harper, 1972); and Andrew Greeley, *Unsecular Man* (New York: Schocken, 1972).

framed in the latter's categories. For the apostle speaking
to the Gentile, it will be communicated in the thought-
forms of that environment. "To the Jews I became like a
Jew, . . . to win Gentiles I made myself one of them" (I
Cor. 9:20, 21 NEB). And the story in our times will be our
story couched in our idiom, clothed in our language.
Evangelists today will take the faith they have found and,
with Peter, fling it joyfully into the air.

But this word does not float ten feet off the ground. It
comes from and returns to the earth. It is a word set
squarely in the midst of a deed. Herein lies the essential
character of apostolic proclamation. Authentic
evangelism is an incarnate word. Hence Acts
evangelism—action evangelism—is "word in deed"
evangelism. It is Peter proclaiming the story in the context
of an authenticating act of shalom. It is neither wordless
deed nor deedless word, but a living union of kerygma
and diakonia. As described in a contemporary statement,
"true Storytelling is Word-in-deed—speaking in the
midst of doing. We testify to salvation not in tent or
temple but *on the road* in our own journeys toward
freedom, justice and peace. We believe *in action
evangelism,* and seek to explore new ways and models of
marrying Word and deed."[5]

One of the failures of conventional evangelism is that it
severs word from deed. This divorce eventuates in partial
conversions. The about-face of the Christian fails to include orientation to the neighbor in need. The medium of
deedless word communicates a message in kind. It is
regrettable that this separation is defended by Donald

---

5. "A Statement of Commitment," *Evangelism for a New Day* (New
York: United Church Board for Homeland Ministries, 1972), pp. 28-29.

McGavran in an otherwise legitimate criticism of an
evangelism of wordless deed: "We must separate
evangelism from other good Christian activities. For example, it has no necessary connection with diakonia
—though diakonia is a fruit of the Spirit and may on
occasion commend the gospel. An intelligent Christian
will notice that diakonia is often a good preparation for
the gospel, but he will note that it was never consciously
so used in the early church."[6] As we can see from the
frequent conjunction of healings and wonders in apostolic evangelism in the Book of Acts, McGavran's claim is
mistaken. Speaking about Peter's healing of the lame man
Barclay observes: "According to the story in Acts, a main
instrument in the converting work of the early preachers
and apostles was the healing work which they were able
to do. It was the healing of the lame man at the Beautiful
Gate of the Temple which set Jerusalem in a ferment and
which the Jewish leaders were quite unable to
deny. . . . David Smith quotes a saying that in those days
these apostolic miracles were the bells which called people into the church."[7] Commenting on the same text
Douglas Webster avers, "It is preaching in context, not *in
vacuo*. . . . It is perfectly clear from the Acts that the apostles regarded the ministry of Christian healing, if offered
as a service in the name of Christ, as part of their
evangelistic activity."[8]

It is surely true that there are occasions in Acts when no
deed is reported as an immediate context for the word

6. In Donald McGavran (ed.), *The Eye of the Storm* (Waco, Tex.:
Word, 1972), p. 64.

7. *Op. cit.*, p. 39.

8. *Op. cit.*, p. 83.

spoken (for example, Philip and the Ethiopian official, Acts 8:26-40), although the history of apostolic acts of shalom does provide a broad servanthood context. And there are genuine and full Christian turnings in the history of mission which result from a word preached *in vacuo*. A sovereign God will not be bound; the divine freedom can choose the way the word will work. But the apostolic way, while not a legalistic methodology, is incarnate evangelism, one in which the enfleshed word is faithfully communicated by kerygma proclaimed in the setting of diakonia. To the telling of the Christian, then and now, God adds "testimony by signs, by miracles, by manifold works of power" (Heb. 2:4 NEB).

Call

Evangelism connects *the* story with *my* story. It strikes home when the divine saga fuses with our own tale. The news is for me, and only becomes a Word when it is heard. That is why evangelism has an existential focus: "Repent then, and turn to God" (Acts 3:19 TEV). Evangelism is a personal call that is truly heard only when the story of human sin becomes the confession of my tale: "God have mercy upon me a sinner!" And it finds its mark when the drama of divine redemption becomes known as persona' gift: "Thanks be to God who gives us the victory throug! our Lord Jesus Christ!" It happens when *conversion* takes place. We shall devote the final chapter to an exploration of this personal turn from darkness and toward the light.

Confrontation

"Peter and John were still speaking to the people when

the priests, the officers in charge of the Temple guards and the Sadducees came up to them" (Acts 4:1 TEV). The act of engaged evangelism provoked the antagonism of the power structure, which in this case was a religious-political-military complex. It swiftly silenced the proclamation. "So they arrested them and put them in jail . . ." (Acts 4:3a TEV).

What causes the ire of the "principalities and powers"? The text indicates two provocations. First is annoyance "because the apostles were teaching the people that Jesus had been raised from death . . ." (Acts 4:2a TEV). The good news that the powers of death had been defeated angered their earthly surrogates. Second, the inquisition the next day conducted by Annas, Caiaphas, John, and Alexander focused on the deed rather than the word: "How did you do this?" (Acts 4:7b TEV). Peter acknowledged the cause of their distress: "If we are being questioned today about the good deed done to the lame man . . ." (Acts 4:9 TEV).

The attack by the principalities and powers is predictable. The good news preached comes as an announcement that the prince of darkness has been defeated, and the world is flooded with the light of the resurrection. Further evidence of this conquest is given in the healing of a broken body. It is no wonder that the rulers of the old age become unnerved. What disturbs them is a word-indeed, the proclamation of the Kingdom's coming in the context of signs of its arrival.

The response of the apostles to the assaults of the powers is instructive. "The members of the Council were amazed to see how bold Peter and John were . . ." (Acts 4:13a TEV). Fearlessness expresses itself initially in the form of a homily delivered in answer to the allegations.

The moment of confrontation itself provides the occasion for kerygma. And so the second evangelism sermon is preached in the setting of resistance to the powers and principalities. And the bold apostles make yet another declaration of freedom in reaction to the warning from the Council to cease their evangelistic activities. "You yourself judge what is right in God's sight, to obey you or to obey God" (Acts 4:19 TEV).

What is being said? The message that comes through is that evangelism antagonizes wickedness in high places. The word that announces the conquest of the powers and the deed that validates this proclamation evoke the wrath of the rulers of this world.[9] Those who "sit in the seats of the mighty" are regularly suspect in the Bible: the nation that exalts itself, the rich who lord it over the poor, the king who enslaves the people, the priest who plays God. Power generates pride. Human sin is such that with the accumulation of power the self is encouraged to think of itself more highly than it ought to think. The ensuing egomania creates pretensions of godlikeness. Thus the powerful are especially susceptible to an idolatry that both challenges God and lords it over other humans. The higher power pyramids, the more dangerous become the pretensions. But the word comes that there is only one God, and that God does not permit the abuse of the lowly by the high and the mighty. "God sits in the heavens and laughs" at the pretensions of the rich and the powerful. And finally "God puts the mighty from their seats and exalts those of low degree. He has filled the hungry with

9. For a discussion of principalities and powers see William String-fellow, *An Ethic for Christians and Other Aliens in a Strange Land* (Waco, Tex.: Word, 1973); Hendrikus Berkhof, *Christ and the Powers* (Scottdale, Pa.: Herald, 1962); and Albert van den Heuvel, *These Rebellious Powers* (New York: Friendship Press, 1965).

good things . . . and the rich he has sent away" (Luke 1:52-53 NEB).

Faithful evangelism that challenges the arrogance of power by word and deed reaps the enmity of the world. The story of Christian Henry Rauch and his evangelistic efforts among native Americans on the Connecticut border is not uncommon in the history of mission. Rauch had come to them from a German Reformed community near Bethlehem, Pennsylvania. As an historian of the last century tells it: "In proportion to the success of this mission among the Indians grew almost a wicked prejudice against it, and opposition to it, among the white settlers of the province. The loss the whites sustained in not having these Indians in their interest, and under their control, as formerly, when they were accustomed to taking unlawful liberties and advantages of them, by defrauding them of their just due for labor, by imposing liquor upon them, thereby encouraging intoxication, for the sake of gain, was considered by them as a serious loss. . . . And ascribing the cause of change in the life and morals of these Indians to the missionaries, they sought by every stratagem to get rid of them. . . . All kinds of false charges were brought against the missionaries. They were accused as being enemies to the government; as being secret papists and traitors; as being in alliance with the French in Canada, to furnish the Indians with arms and ammunition to fight the English. In December, 1744, they were brought before the magistrate, for examination, and still later they were cited to appear before the governor himself. . . . At length such oppressive laws were passed in reference to them, and such restrictions laid upon them, that they could no longer carry forward their missionary work. In the beginning of the year 1745, they

were compelled reluctantly to leave the converted Indians to themselves. A sad parting followed; and Mr.
Rauch and his companions, not without receiving insults
from the mobs on the route, found their way back to
Bethlehem."[10]

Growth

The readiness to encounter the principalities and powers was a feature of the mission theology of the 1960s. It
emerged among renewal-oriented laity and clergy in the
struggles for civil rights and minority justice, in Third-
World and women's liberation movements, and in the
environmental crusade. Associated with this new consciousness was another conviction, which often appeared when "the enemy" seemed to be carrying the day,
that "God wants us to be faithful, not successful."[11] This
slogan became the consolation of many clergy whose
congregations deteriorated numerically as a result of their
involvement in and preoccupation with human rights or
peace activity. And it served as the ecclesiology for many
laity who retired to small house or underground churches
in the belief that the lackluster record of conventional
congregations proved them to be faithless. This mood
persists in the 1970s, when it may take the form of an
attempt to recover the sect principle or adopt a "theology
of waiting." Or it may appear in the conception of the
church as a random event of faithfulness in or outside of
organized religion.

10. Henry Harbaugh, *The Fathers of the German Reformed Church
in Europe and America,* I (Lancaster: Sprenger & Westhaeffer, 1857),
383-84.

11. For a discussion of the mission premises of an earlier era see my
essay "The Crisis of the Congregation: A Debate," in Robertson (ed.),
Voluntary Associations, pp. 275-97.

It is surely true that there are moments in the life of the people of God when the theme of the remnant is appropriate, when the powers of evil run riot and faithlessness sweeps over the church establishment. But if we judge the meaning of mission by the Acts happenings, we can see that this is not a motif which can be inflated into a full-blown theology of evangelism. Indeed, the apostles "failed" with the powers and principalities, but they succeeded with the people. In the very midst of alienation from the powers that be, an engaged evangelism evoked remarkable response in other quarters: "Many who heard the message believed . . . and the number of men came to about five thousand" (Acts 4:4 TEV).

As the word made flesh brought the church into existence, so a word-in-deed continues to draw people into the body of Christ. We do not apologize for the belief that when the good news is told and done, when the seed is planted, there will be some fertile soil in which "God gives the growth."

And why would this not be so? Since the world is Christic, bathed in a new light, there will be those who see that horizon glow. Since the world is different, it is to be anticipated that the evangelist will not only be an agent of wonders of physical healing, but also the enabler of signs of spiritual wholeness. The Spirit of the new day of the Lord is upon us; and the powerful working of that Spirit in our midst will show its evidence in changed lives. Authentic evangelism is effective evangelism.

The populist leaning of the Bible is illustrated by the tendency of its effectiveness to be with "little people." The obverse of the biblical suspicion of the high and the mighty is its identification with the humble and the lowly. The Teacher who said that it is "easier for a camel to pass through the eye of a needle than for a rich man to enter the kingdom of God" (Matt. 19:24 NEB) also said "blessed are you poor, for yours is the kingdom of God" (Luke 6:20 RSV). This bias in favor of ordinary and oppressed citizenry is reflected in both the evangelists and the evangelized of the Acts account. The elite were surprised to learn that Peter and John both were "ordinary men with no education" (Acts 4:13a TEV). It is such ordinary humans who were used by the Holy Spirit to draw a great number of others of their kind into the ranks of the church.

The possibility of church growth is a new thought for many of the bruised missioners of the 1960s. Whether apostolic effectiveness is a persuasive model may depend on how they read the contemporary historical context, as well as how they read the biblical text. Contributing to a defeatist missiology in the United States is the conventional wisdom of the 1960s regarding middle America. If Archie Bunker is viewed as an irrevocable enemy of the poor, the young, and the black, it is predictable that a sect ecclesiology which excommunicates middle America will emerge. But what if this is an inaccurate social analysis? Suppose that middle Americans are also victims? Suppose that the unyoung, the unpoor, the unblack are potential allies of the young, the poor, and the black? The evidence of this populist thesis continues to mount in the years of Watergate, the continuing and accelerating environmental and energy crisis, the perils of economic and political royalism.[12] My own conviction about

12. The literature includes Robert Coles and Jon Erikson, *The Middle Americans* (Boston: Atlantic/Little, Brown, 1971); Richard Parker, *The Myth of the Middle Class* (New York: Liveright, 1972); Richard Sennet and Jonathan Cobb, *The Hidden Injuries of Class* (New York: Knopf, 1972); Jack Newfield and Jeff Greenfield, *A Populist Manifesto* (New York: Praeger, 1972); Kenneth Lasson, with an afterword by Ralph Nader, *The Workers* (New York: Grossman, 1971); Fred Harris, *The New Populism* (New York: Saturday Review Press, 1973); Morton Mintz and Jerry Cohen, with an introduction by Ralph Nader, *America, Inc.* (New York: Dell, 1971).

evangelism has developed concurrently with the growth of my awareness of the plight of middle America.[13] To understand that the hates of Archie Bunker may be related to his hurts is to see middle Americans as humans in need. And to perceive that humanity is to open oneself to a mission to middle America, one that seeks to win Archie and to exorcise his demons. Mission to this constituency goes on from a position of alongsided-ness rather than over-against-ness. It may be that populism and evangelism are important companion commitments in the 1970s.

In protest against a defeatist missiology, an evangelism perspective developed in the late 1960s which was determined to recover the theme of "church growth."[14] Disagreeing with the pietists, church growth protagonists view evangelism as more than a surfeit of feeling; evangelism entails institutional concern and enlargement. And disagreeing with the activists, they see the test of mission as the conversion of persons rather than the involvement of the church in contemporary social issues. Their institutional realism and understanding of evangelism as anticipating growth are commendable. However, church growth theory does not strike clearly enough the notes either of healing or of challenge. While "service" is included as a result of evangelism, the apostolic deed is not seen as a constitutive factor of evangelism. Nor is there any lifting up of the costly encounter with structures of evil, in which the evangelist is

13. Themes developed in my *Liberation in Middle America* (Philadelphia: Pilgrim Press, 1971); and *Do and Tell*, pp. 63-78.

14. For a bibliography see McGavran, *op. cit.*, pp. 297-99. Key interpretations are McGavran, *Understanding Church Growth* (Grand Rapids: Eerdmans, 1969); and Allen Tippett, *Church Growth and the Word of God* (Grand Rapids: Eerdmans, 1970).

prepared to stand before the powers that be and confess, "We must obey God rather than men." Church growth as the decisive rationale for evangelism is prey to the temptation of muting the controversial word and deed which are intrinsic to the evangelism act. An era of engagement with the powers will not let us forget Bonhoeffer's insight that evangelism means participating in God's sufferings in the world. How to retain that forthright wrestle with the rulers of this age and at the same time extend the invitation to those outside the church and encourage the celebration of the growth of the church is a special challenge to contemporary evangelism.[15]

Life Together

"See how these Christians love one another!" According to Tertullian, this was a common observation about the early Christian community. The quality of life within the church was part of the evangelistic message of the church. Michael Green notes: "They made the grace of God credible by a society of love and mutual care which astonished the pagans and was recognized as something entirely new. It lent persuasiveness to their claim that the New Age had dawned in Christ."[16] It is no accident, therefore, that part of the evangelism rhythm we have been tracing is the statement that "the group of believers was one in heart and mind" (Acts 4:32 TEV). Evangelism includes the witness and life of a caring community. Koinonia belongs alongside kerygma and diakonia. To-

15. For a thoughtful assessment of church growth theory see Costas, *The Church and Its Mission,* pp. 87-149.

16. Michael Green, *Evangelism in the Early Church* (Grand Rapids: Eerdmans, 1970), p. 120. See also Webster, *op. cit.,* pp. 130-40; Hendrik Kraemer, *The Communication of the Christian Faith* (Philadelphia: Westminster, 1956), pp. 40ff.

gether they constitute an enfleshed evangelical word.

As the evangelism thrust of the early church begins with a deed of love, it also ends with one. The first is an external and the second an internal act. Both express the neighbor love that reaches out to those in need, and as such both constitute eschatological signs and wonders that surround and authenticate the proclamation of good news. The shalom within the Christian community marks it as a colony of the future, an earnest of the Kingdom which is to come.

The New Testament refers time and again to special characteristics of Christian koinonia that identify it as a sign of the Kingdom. In Christ "there is no such thing as Jew and Greek, slave and freeman, male and female" (Gal. 3:28 NEB). In this community the usual alienations and distinctions do not apply. There is love and care for the widow, the orphan, the stranger, the poor, the prisoner. The wretched of the earth, the outcasts, the dysfunctional receive special attention. The reconciliation of the estranged, the dignifying of the oppressed, and the honoring of the outcast demonstrate the divine love that goes out not merely to the lovable and worthy, but to the unlovely and socially worthless.[17] Here on earth there is a place where one can taste the liberation and reconciliation for which the world is intended and which it is promised.

Life together is by no means limited to "spiritual" caring for one another. It is down-to-earth and forthrightly physical. Thus "no one said that any of his belongings was his own, but all shared with one another everything

17. See Helmut Thielicke, *Nihilism* (tr. John Doberstein) (New York: Harper, 1961); and Luigi Civardi, *Christianity and Social Justice* (New York: Academy Library Guild, 1962).

they had. . . . Those who owned fields or houses would
sell them, bring the money received from the sale, and
turn it over to the apostles; and the money was distributed
to each one according to his need" (Acts 4:32b, 34-35
TEV). Anyone who held back from the full sharing of
goods and property came under sharp condemnation
(Acts 5:11). Thus the bodily and material gifts and imperatives of the Kingdom demonstrated by the healing of the
lame man at the opening of Acts 3 are matched by the
bodily and material ministry within the body of Christ at
the close of the evangelism sequence.

Part of the life together of early Christian communities
was the constant celebration of their source. After Peter
and John returned to the group to report the missionary
happenings, "they all joined together in prayer to
God. . . . When they finished praying, the place where
they were meeting was shaken. They were all filled with
the Holy Spirit and began to speak God's message with
boldness" (Acts 4:24, 31 TEV). Prayer, praise, and
preaching were to be found at the heart of the body. And
the center of this worship life was the sacramental meal.
The deeds and words of testimony were offered up to God
and became themselves a witness to the Kingdom that
had broken into their midst. Thus leitourgia is part and
parcel of Christian koinonia; worship is joined to life
together.

What does the primitive church's common life have to
teach the evangelist today? The lesson is that no
evangelism journey is complete without a house of hospitality. The witness of a loving and celebrating Christian
congregation is a necessary partner to proclamation, invitation, prophecy, growth, and acts of mercy to the
stranger. Those won by the good news have to be re-

ceived into the community whose life together looks
something like the commonwealth to which the
evangelist points. In fact, this community will be a deed
that calls attention to the word, as well as the authenticating of that word once heard by others. The being of the
Kingdom in the midst of those who testify to it is the seal of
its arrival and power.

Does desire for this kind of koinonia mean that the
church today must imitate the "primitive communism" of
the New Testament communities? ("Primitive communism" in the broadest sense, since the early Christian
churches did not collectivize the means of production as
in Marxism and related socialist theory and practice. But
a radical sharing did take place according to the goal "to
each according to his need.") Biblicism, as a theological
method, would insist on the necessity of replicating the
New Testament model in our evangelism practice. However, the text of the storybook must be brought into conversation with the long history of the church's interpretation and practice, and our own experience of the Spirit.
As in the miracle of healing, so in this miracle of together-
ness, faithfulness to the text is not a wooden repetition of
it. Rather we are challenged by it to find a life together in
the church that comes alive in the light of learnings from
Christian history and contemporary human experience.

Koinonia happens in the church today when a congregation is a support system for the forgotten, de-
humanized, wounded, and dysfunctional. Do the poor,
the black, and the young find a house of hospitality and
full human dignity in the church of the 1970s? Does
Archie Bunker, who feels like no more than a button
number at the mill gate and the forgotten man of a technocratic culture, get back his name and his face in the

Christian congregation? Do women who suffer from sexist social structures find that they are accorded in the
church the decision-making power and full humanity to
which their citizenship in shalom entitles them? Is the
church a place where the aged, living along the margins
of society and declared by that society to be unproduc-
tive, play a responsible role and achieve humanity in the
Christian community?

To take seriously the physical as well as the spiritual
ministry to and with those unloved persons forced to the
edges of society is to attend to the structural aspects of
dehumanization as these can be ministered to within the
church. This is more than giving out Christmas baskets. It
means dealing within the church with elemental needs of
humanization. The benevolent ministries to the elderly
and to the sick, food co-operatives, industrial training,
housing, care of the unwanted and orphan have all taken
on institutional form in the life of the church. Economic
experiments in sharing have also contributed to this long
history.

Part of the internal humanization mandated includes
bringing the church's own traditional structures into line
with its vision. Thus the ordination of women and the
elimination of sexist language in theology and liturgy are
ways of taking seriously the shalom in which there shall
be neither male nor female. The enlargement of the role
of the young and old and of minority groups in the coun-
cils of decision-making also represent earthly ways of
according the full dignity of the commonwealth to those
who live in its colony here and now. In all these ways and
many others, the church of today can bear witness in its
own life to the story it tells, and thus *be* the story in such a
way that others will say, "See how these Christians love
one another!"

"Provival"

From first to last evangelism is future-oriented. Its
ground and goal is shalom, the reconciliation of all
things—humanity and deity, neighbor and neighbor,
neighbor and nature, nation and nation, the world and
God. Its deeds of love at the beginning and end of the
evangelism rhythm are signs and earnests of the coming
Kingdom.

From an eschatological reference point Jürgen Moltmann challenges the conventional idea of *re*volution,
*re*newal, and *re*form.[18] As "re"-turns to a previous state of
affairs from which the world is presumed to have fallen,
these represent a past orientation. As a replay of what has
been, they are not open to the future. In the place of
revolution, Moltmann puts "*pro*volution," a genuine
openness to the not yet, a yearning for the new world God
will bring, one which now we can only see through a
glass darkly.

The evangelism counterpart to "provolution" is
"*pro*vival." Unlike *re*vival, it is not concerned to recover
an experience believed to be lost. Rather, it pursues a
dream which is yet to be of a world that God will bring in,
where the wolf will lie down with the lamb, swords will
be beaten into plowshares, the blind will see, the lame
will walk, the hungry will be fed, the prisoners liberated.
Witness to that great shalom involves empowerment by
the Spirit of the new age to do deeds of shalom. "Provival" is setting up signs in this world to the world to come,
doing miracles of healing and hope. Acts evangelism is an
exercise in "provival."

18. Jürgen Moltmann, *Religion, Revolution and the Future* (tr. M.
Douglas Meeks) (New York: Scribners, 1969), pp. 19-41.

"Provival" is also, in its expectation, whetted for the new, the unforeseen, and the impossible, an orientation to the "Novum." Peter and the apostles were resourceless. They had no money and little education. Yet they were instruments of God able to do and tell in marvelous ways. So "provival" today is the expectation that God will again use the weak and despised things of the world to do miracles of word and deed.

"Provival," in contrast to revival, is not an attempt to rehabilitate those already in the church, to "revive us again." Rather, it moves outside the gates of the temple, risking encounter with situations and people beyond the borders of the church, facing into unchartered, unsafe terrain, looking for new worlds to conquer.

The courage to look ahead instead of backwards comes from the glimpse of the future which "provivalists" receive in Jesus Christ. Paradoxically, this past event provides the aperture through which that future can be seen, and it sets up in the evangelist the yearning, not for what has been, but for what will be.[19] Maranatha—"Come, Lord Jesus"—out of the future to be present with us in the words and deeds of evangelical hope.

Answering the Call

How hard it is to move with Christ into an open future. We like the security of things known. Clinging to the rock of what has been manifests itself in evangelism by the inclination to do those things with which we are familiar,

19. Thus Johannes Metz speaks of the "dangerous memories of Jesus Christ. They break through the canon of what prevails everywhere as self-evident. . . . They are memories we have to reckon with, memories, as it were, with future content." "The Future Ex Memoria Passionis," in Ewert Cousins (ed.), *Hope and the Future of Man* (Philadelphia: Fortress, 1972), p. 126.

which come naturally, which we know. So evangelism is regularly reduced to our own agendas, and becomes grinding our own axes. Reductionism results when doers cry halt to the evangelism process at the point of the deed alone. For them evangelism is the act of mercy and no more. Juxtaposed to doers, but actually of the same mind, are one-dimensional tellers. For them evangelism is solely proclamation. Companions in oversimplification are the callers, those for whom the invitation to the experience of personal salvation is the sum and substance of evangelism. So, too, the confronter, for whom the heat of conflict and suffering become the heart of witness. Still others are beguiled by growth as the one string on the evangelist's bow, viewing recruitment of new members as the be-all and end-all of evangelism. And for still others the life together of the Christian community, its warmth and care, constitute the way and meaning of getting out the good news. Each has discovered an ingredient of Acts evangelism. Each has a gift to bring. But as the body is made up of many parts, so the articulation of the good news is a dynamism that engages all the gifts. To see evangelism in its wholeness, sharing the full gospel in the full orb of doing, telling, calling, confronting, growing, and being is the claim on us made by the first evangelists.

The Word and Deed of God

The acts of the apostles are grounded in the deeds of God. The evangelism rhythm found in the texts just examined has its roots in the divine action itself, as it works in history and as it comes to its quintessential expression in Jesus Christ. Christ the Evangel is the prototype of the evangelist. Each of the six motifs found in Acts evangelism also occurs in his ministry.

(1) The "good deed done to a lame man" by Peter and John had its genesis in the healings of Jesus. In Christ the empowerment to act comes from the inbreaking of the Kingdom of God. Jesus "saw Satan fall like lightning" and knew of the release of the power of the future in the midst of present physical agony. That power of the shalom-to-be was at work in him as "by the finger of God . . . he cast out demons." The glimpse of the future, seen in the power released through the firstfruits, became a fertile field springing up in the healing ministry of Peter and John. Between Jesus' reach toward human brokenness and the apostles stood Calvary and Easter. At that latter time the final resistance, the last enemy, met its match and was overcome. The power found in Jesus was now poured out on the apostolic community to do "even greater things. . . ."[20]

(2) Jesus came to testify as well as to heal, to tell as well as to do. He was called to preach good news to the poor, as well as to give sight to the blind and set free the oppressed. There was a word to be spoken as well as a deed to be done. That word was the good news of the coming of the Kingdom of God. It was the announcement that the future was rolling up on the shores of the present, and the prayerful pointing to the fulfilment when the Kingdom would come and God's will would be done on earth as it is in heaven.

(3) The invasion of the commonwealth of God, and the witness to it in word and deed, laid a personal imperative on those who heard about it and saw its evidence: "Repent and believe the gospel" (Mark 1:15 NEB). Once

20. The literature on this theme runs from such biblical studies as Amos Wilder, *The Eschatology and Ethics of Jesus* to Wolfhart Pannenberg's *Theology and the Kingdom of God.*

again the apostles' invitation to turn to the light is anticipated in the personal call Jesus issues. "The people that
live in darkness have seen a great light; the light dawned
on the dwellers in the land of death's dark
shadow. . . . Repent; for the kingdom of Heaven is upon
you" (Matt. 4:16, 17 NEB).

(4) The powers of darkness raged at the word and
deed. Wickedness in high places took offense at the
proclamation and action which challenged their
suzerainty. The religious, political, and military power
structures determined that their authority would not be
undermined by the subversive claims and signs of a new
Kingdom. Thus the persecution of the apostles is anticipated in the crucifixion of Christ.

(5) While the powers and principalities were stirred to
anger and aggression, the people came to hear and to be
healed. The word-in-deed fell on some good soil, and
growth happened. But there were brambles and rocky
ground as well. The quick growth in shallow earth soon
made itself apparent when the crowd disappeared. The
church to be born had to wait upon the climactic events
of Calvary and resurrection. Here lies the difference between the pre-Easter and post-Easter responses. The pre-
Easter growth was the gathering of the seeds of the
church, the formation of a company of disciples. The
flowering took place in the Acts evangelism of the apostles.

(6) The life together of that company of disciples was
the harbinger of the primitive church's sharing and caring. Their common life, both in its physical and spiritual
dimensions, is symbolized and enacted in the upper
room. Here there is bread, wine, and prayer. The first
Eucharist is a foretaste of the koinonia and leitourgia of
the Acts community.

Doing, telling, calling, confronting, growing, being —the rays of Acts evangelism have their source in the horizon Light.

The primal word-in-deed ingredients of action evangelism and their expression in the ministry of Jesus can be driven back even further to their fount in the Christian story itself. In that tale, *God does what God is.* God is a God who acts. Hence, the Christian faith is a saga of the deeds of God from creation to consummation.

At the same time that story tells us that *God says what God does.* The interpretation of the action of God is part and parcel of the unfolding drama. The seer, the prophet, points to what is happening in the light of the visions disclosed. The word of God is conjoined to the deeds of God.

The marriage of word and deed is consummated in the birth of Jesus Christ. Here the word is made flesh. The converging lines of action and interpretation meet at the incarnation. The Word of God becomes the Deed of God. It is out of this fusion that the ministry of Jesus comes. And from it proceed the Acts evangelism of the apostles, and the word-in-deed mandates and miracles of today's evangelists.

CHAPTER FIVE

Conversion

The note of conversion is muted in contemporary theology. When professional theologians are preoccupied with the erosion of transcendence, college departments of religious studies feature courses in Zen, and denominations give priority to the "faith crisis," the claims of Christian turning become predictably marginal.

Nevertheless, there are new sounds to be heard. Paradoxically they come from those active at the boundary of church and world and immersed in the struggles for humanization. Third World theologian Gustavo Gutierrez underscores the relation of liberation to conversion.[1] Robert McAfee Brown observes that "the death-of-God theologians said that faith and hope were gone, and all that was left was a theology of love. Then the Germans told us that the big task was to recover a theology of hope. Maybe tomorrow's job will be to recover a theology of faith. . . ."[2] Roger Shinn, defending "political theology,"

1. Gustavo Gutierrez, *A Theology of Liberation,* pp. 269-71.

2. Robert McAfee Brown, "Discoveries and Dangers," in A. Geyer & D. Peerman (eds.), *Theological Crossings* (Grand Rapids: Eerdmans, 1971), p. 22.

makes a plea for joining it with personal conscious-ness-transformation.[3] And "consciousness-raising" in the movements for women's liberation strikes chords rem-iniscent of classical conversion.

The reflection that follows has grown out of participa-tion in an activist church which has over the past few years edged the "faith crisis" toward "faith exploration" and finally into "evangelism" (to use the name of United Church of Christ programs). This movement toward faith affirmation has, however, together with Gutierrez, Brown, and Shinn, refused to bow the knee to the latest Baal, an other-worldly religiosity, and has sought instead to hold together the humanization commitments of the 1960s with the religious quests of the 1970s. But the practice of Acts evangelism presses home the question, what is the new life born from this fertile word-in-deed? What is the fruit that comes from an evangelical womb? Involvement in action evangelism has propelled to the foreground the issue of conversion.

Words

Commentary on conversion often focuses on the *experience* of it, either subjectively, as in E. Stanley Jones' *Conversion*, or as an object of research as in William James' *Varieties of Religious Experience*. We choose to begin at another point. As with Christian doctrine in general, so also with the intimate appropriations of faith, our experience must come under the scrutiny of key events and perceptions in the Christian tale. If authentic, my personal story (the experiential) will confirm these events and perceptions, but it is also subject to distortions

3. Roger Shinn, "Political Theology in the Cross Fire," *Journal of Current Social Issues*, X, No. 2 (Spring 1972), 18-20.

introduced by my agenda and conditioning. The interiorizing of piety, its disjunction from the institutional issues of both church and world, a phenomenon often found in conversion talk, is an example of this. Thus, my story and the church's storytelling must take their bearings from the primal story. We reach for that tale in the storybook. A responsible hermeneutic will then bring Scripture into conversation with tradition and contemporary experience (as in our earlier discussion of storybook, storytellers, and storyland) in a search for today's rendering of the meaning of conversion.

There are several Greek terms used to talk about the conversion happenings of the New Testament: *epistrephein, strephein, metanoein.* Their Hebrew counterpart is *shubh.*[4] What is common to these words, both in their general cultural usage (in the Bible and in the community at large) and in their transfer to a "religious" context, is the theme of turning. We have to do in conversion with an about-face, a reorientation, a change of direction, a fresh tack. When these words appear in the context of the kerygma and its call for response, the reorientation represents a first and fundamental turnabout. Christian conversion is, therefore, a threshold commitment, a new posture, a new attitude for the journey to follow, a new beginning. In Erik Routley's terms, "It means stopping, turning, attending and pursuing a new course."[5]

As the word "attitude" is used today for the physical

4. For some perceptive word studies see Charles Edwin Carlston, *Metanoia and Church Discipline* (unpubl. Harvard Ph.D. thesis, 1959); William Holladay, *The Root Subh in the Old Testament* (Leiden: Brill, 1958).

5. Erik Routley, *The Gift of Conversion* (Philadelphia: Muhlenberg, 1955), p. 32.

angle of a trajectory, so, too, the Greek turning words are
not limited to inner attitudes of mind, but include physical positioning as well. Especially is this true of the dominant word *epistrephein* when applied to the drama of
Christian turning. William Barclay observes: "The basic
meaning of *epistrephein* is a turning around either in the
physical or the mental or the spiritual sense of the term;
and thus when the word moves in the world of thought
and religion, it means a change of outlook and a new
direction of life and action."[6] Christian conversion is a
radically and totally new posture, the changing of one's
feet, relationships, and behavior as well as one's mind
and heart. This encompassing quality of turning is stressed
by Nock in his contrast between Christian turning and
general religious "adhesion."[7] Adhesion is the label-
changing that characterizes Gnostic and mystery cult
devotees who are drawn to new religions by the titilla-
tions of esoteric knowledge or by needs to be coped with.
Conversion in the early church is not a change of clothes
along the old route, but a drastic about-face by a new
creature going in a new direction. Michael Green is even
more emphatic: "Conversion, then, in our sense of an
exclusive change of faith, of ethic, of cult was indeed
utterly foreign to the mentality of the Graeco-Roman
world."[8] These assertions parallel Bonhoeffer's distinction between "religion," that universal hunger for a god-
of-the-gaps to take care of the ills of the flesh and the cares
of the world, and Christian faith, in which the believer is
led by grace to keep company with the sufferings of God

6. William Barclay, *Turning to God*, p. 20.

7. Arthur Darby Nock, *Conversion* (London: Oxford U. P., 1933),
pp. 7f.

8. Michael Green, *Evangelism in the Early Church*, p. 146.

in the world.[9] Conversion marks Christianity, therefore, as a demanding *moral* religion whose entry point requires a decisive turn, a rigorous internal and external reorientation.

Images

There is a set of New Testament images, in addition to these words, which both helps us to understand biblical conversion and interpret it today: light and darkness. Reflecting on his own Damascus road encounter with "a light brighter than the sun," Paul hears this evangelical mandate: "I send you to open their eyes and turn them from darkness to light, and from the dominion of Satan to God. . ." (Acts 26:18a NEB). The association of light with conversion is very common in Christian history. It appears in Augustine's description of his own turning, and in Cyprian's testimony of his conversion (at baptism).[10] Douglas Webster recounts a typical contemporary experience of new birth permeated with light imagery, [11] and Erik Routley exegetes the seeing of blind Bartimaeus as a paradigm of conversion.[12] As we found light images helpful in setting forth the larger story in Chapter 2, we return to them in the examination of the end result of storytelling and doing.

Texts

We have a word (turning) and an image (light) to provide

9. I have treated this theme in *Humiliation and Celebration*, pp. 91-122.

10. W.P. Paterson, *Conversion* (New York: Scribners, 1940), p. 78.

11. Webster, *What Is Evangelism?*, pp. 164ff.

12. Routley, *op. cit.*, pp. 41-54. Cf. Barth's interesting description of Paul's conversion (*Church Dogmatics*, IV. 3, pp. 198-211).

initial reference points for exploring conversion. Let us proceed another step into the biblical materials. These data include Peter's Pentecostal sermon, with its injunction "Turn away from your sins, each one of you, be baptized in the name of Jesus Christ so your sins will be forgiven: and you will receive God's gift of the Holy Spirit" (Acts 2:38 TEV); the important Acts cycle explored earlier with its call, "Repent then and turn to God, so that your sins may be wiped out" (Acts 3:19 NEB); "Then God has given to the Gentiles also the opportunity to repent and live" (Acts 11:18 TEV); "The power of the Lord was with them, and a great many became believers, and turned to the Lord" (Acts 11:21 NEB); "I preached that they must repent of their sins and turn to God, and do the things which should show they had repented" (Acts 26:20 TEV); "All these people speak of how you received us when we visited you, and how you turned away from idols to God, to serve the true and living God . . ." (I Thess. 1:9-10 TEV); and Jesus' foundational call "Repent and believe the gospel" (Mark 1:15 NEB).

As the characteristics of this threshold commitment unfold in these stories and challenges, it becomes clear that New Testament conversion is *not* something that happens in the twinkling of an eye. Revivalists whose stock in trade is the emotional pressure to twist a decision out of a listener regularly portray turning as instantaneous. About this Barclay remarks, "It can never be said of the early Church that its preachers depended on anything like a kind of mass emotionalism."[13] He argues for a New Testament "educational evangelism," represented by the dialogue and argument in which Paul engaged, rather than what Horace Bushnell called "concussion conver-

13. Barclay, *op. cit.*, p. 38.

sion." New Testament turning was a process, not a neatly
packaged product wrapped up in an evening under a tent.
Like the process of being born, a familiar conversion
figure, it involves labor and it takes time. To return to our
earlier image, doing an about-face, we might say that the
turn is composed of a series of "turning points." Total
turning includes a sequence of smaller turns, stages on a
new life's way.

Four turning points are called for in the texts: "repent,"
"believe," "be baptized," "serve." Authentic Christian
reorientation is a full turn that includes each. If one or
another is omitted, there may be a turning of sorts, but
instead of being "on the right track" the individual goes
off at an angle, stumbling into the shadows, losing touch
with the horizon that lies out ahead.

Repent

Repent! What image does that suggest? A gaunt sign-
wielder walking down the city streets calling down doom
on a sick society? A hellfire and damnation preacher
shaking the tent poles with his roars? Billy Graham looking out of a television set and pointing his finger at you?
There is a far more profound meaning to repentance than
any of these pictures portrays.

The New Testament word for repentance is *metanoia*.
In the key sequence of evangelism motifs in Acts 3, it
appears on the heels of an apostolic word and deed that
testified to the new age which had burst in upon the world
in Jesus' victory over the powers of darkness. So it is also
located in the Pentecostal preaching of Peter, in Paul's
understanding of his commission to turn the people from
darkness to light, and in the proclamation of Jesus him-

self, "The kingdom of God is upon you, repent . . ."
(Mark 1:15 NEB).

As in the larger movement of conversion, the meaning
is again "turn." But there is a special nuance. Barclay
observes that a turn involves "a turning from something
and a turning towards something."[14] Carlston refines this
further: "If any distinction is to be made between
metanoein and *epistrephein* in the New Testament, it is
that *metanoein* emphasizes somewhat more strongly the
element of turning away from the old, *epistrephein*
turning toward the new (cf. Acts 3:10; 26:20)."[15] John R.
W. Stott makes a similar distinction: "Now both repentance and faith are described in Acts in terms of 'turning.'
Repentance is a turning from wickedness (3:26) whereas
faith is a turning 'to God' (15:19, 26:20). . . ."[16]
Metanoia, therefore, we interpret to be the "turning away
from" movement of conversion.

What are we called to turn from? "The dominion of
darkness." What lurks in these shadows? In Colossians it
is the power of Satan. In Thessalonians it is idols. In short
we are in bondage to the powers of darkness. We have
been enticed to face about from the light and have eyes
only for the shadowside of the world. These forces of
darkness that exercise control over human lives run, in
the New Testament, from very intimate deities (Paul re-
bukes those "whose god is their belly") to vast world-
ranging, empire-building principalities and powers, the
Caesars who demand complete fealty.

What is today's counterpart of this biblical notion?

14. *Ibid.*, p. 26.

15. Carlston, *op. cit.*, p. 141.

16. J.R.W. Stott, *The Meaning of Evangelism* (London: Falcon
Booklets, 1964), p.14.

What holds people captive in this time and place? The gods are everywhere. The intimate enemies and personal idolatries include bondage to drugs, racism, power, lust, sexism, sports, cars, television, and torpor. These are the private demons that have to be exorcised. There are also public powers that hold sway over us, modern Caesars who claim hegemony. They include political tyrannies, economic baronies, military systems, technocratic juggernauts, structures of racial injustice, dehumanizing educational designs. William Stringfellow has deftly sketched both the biblical characterizations and the contemporary manifestations of these "powers of death."[17]

Yet these ominous forces do not have the last word. The good news is that the powers of death have lost their sting. The captors have been captured, the slavemasters defeated. The gods have been mortally wounded and in time they shall be dead. Christ the Light enters the dominion of darkness at Bethlehem, engages in combat with the demonic in Galilee, suffers the final assaults of the foe on Calvary, and triumphs over the last enemy on Easter morning. Now that light radiates our historical horizon. The Christic dawn heralds a new day. Therefore, repent! That is to say, shake loose! The strength has gone out of the grip the demonic private and public powers have on you. Night is over. The powers of darkness have been defeated. You *are* free: now be what you are—be free!

This is the good news of liberation. It changes things. For those in personal bondage, the message of deliverance breaks the chains of drugs and promiscuity, power and glory. Repentance means wrenching loose from these personal powers in the knowledge that Christ has

17. Stringfellow, *An Ethic for Christians and Other Aliens in a Strange Land,* pp. 77-114.

set us free from their regency. Here we honor the changed life of a "Jesus person" whose heroin habit has met its match in the power of Jesus to make things new. For those in public bondage the message of deliverance shatters the manacles of the oppressor, the political, economic, and social tyrannies. Here we celebrate the liberation faith of a Third World Christian who knows that the roar and posturing of a military junta is the death rattle of a frightened god, that obeisance before this swaggering deity is to be repented of, and that the victory of Christ is to be lived out in resistance to the powers of evil.

Repentance, therefore, in its fundamental sense, is not the simplistic finger-wagging moralism into which it regularly gets transformed. It is the invitation to be free, to turn away from captivity to the darkness because the power of that darkness has been broken. If Christ has made you free, you are free indeed.

Deliverance from one bondage may not be the end of the matter. We are all prone to polytheism. We worship more than one idol. The Jesus person, preoccupied with announcing the defeat of his drug demon, may fail to see other captivities to which he is prey. The sad story of inner conquest is that it may too easily tolerate political and economic oppression at the same time. It must be taught that Christ is Lord over Caesars as well as souls. Here the liberation Christian has testimony to share with the Jesus person. But the reverse is also true, for preoccupation with political and economic liberation may obscure the personal demons to which reformers and revolutionaries may still be captive, much to the disservice of their reformations and revolutions.

Repentance, therefore, is not moralism, oblivious to the perils of the demonic and Christian freedom from it.

But it *is* moral. The act of repentance also includes painful acknowledgment of our accountability. The false gods have tempted us, lured us, hypnotized us, imprisoned us, but it is we who have acceded to their allurements. It is we who have been meekly led into captivity. We are guilty.

For some time it has been thought impolite to speak about our guilt. Karl Menninger in his timely study *Whatever Became of Sin?* argues for the restoration of "sin" to both the language and thought structures of modern society. He reminds us that few generations have had the fact of human self-serving made so clear as ours. The titanic moral evils of the contemporary world cannot be swept under the rug by clever behaviorisms or sociological excuses or even sophisticated theologizing. The powers of darkness hold us in bondage because we allow ourselves to be enslaved that way.[18] The Genesis saga says it better than our abstractions: while the Devil may be the occasion for our fall, he tempts us to "be as gods." Thus the ultimate idolatry is not the worship of other gods, but the adoration of ourselves. We bend the knee to the powers of darkness because of what they promise to do for our own self-aggrandizement. To repent, therefore, is to acknowledge our own personal complicity in turning to the dark. It is the painful admission of guilt, the plea for mercy to blot out sin.

Just as the good news of the coming Kingdom is a prelude to the repentant act of breaking free from demonic powers, so it is also the preface to a penitent admission of our complicity in that former slave state. In the first instance, the dawn comes as gift; in the second as mandate. To understand our guilt we must have a vision

18. Karl Menninger, *Whatever Became of Sin?* (New York: Hawthorn, 1973).

of what we were made for. The law of love, the way of
shalom, is the schoolmaster that trains us in what we have
done to that dream. The life and death of Christ as the
presence of that future in our history lures us toward the
vision. We know we should be as he is. Yet for those
brought to their knees in repentance, that same vision
judges as well as lures. "The good that I want to do, I fail
to do; but what I do is the wrong which is against my
will. . . . Miserable creature that I am, who is there to
rescue me. . . ?" (Rom. 7:19, 20, 24a NEB).

Being captured by the vision, having a will to do the
good, plunging into a life of good works are preparatory
to the Pauline understanding of our moral ambiguity.
Visionaries are positioned to ask the right questions. Penitent visionaries *do*. To Bonhoeffer's "only those who
obey believe"[19] we must add, "Only those who obey,
repent."

A long theological tradition from Augustine through
Kierkegaard to Reinhold Niebuhr has reminded us that
our vulnerability to sin is commensurate with the two
dimensions of our personhood: our freedom and our
finitude, our transcendence and our contingency. We
succumb on the one hand to the perversities of an arrogance
that is parasitic on freedom. And on the other we are
vulnerable to an apathy that grafts itself upon our finitude:
pride and sloth. In one case, we lord it over others. In the
other, we flee from the struggle, seeking escape from
freedom. And these lethal tendencies are themselves mirror images of the idols we worship. The gods of racism,
sexism, and nationalism infect us with hubris; other
deities invite us into a lassitude that leaves decisions for

19. Dietrich Bonhoeffer, *The Cost of Discipleship* (New York:
Macmillan, 1960), pp. 48-68.

the future to the "snake."[20] But at the bottom of our
tendency to prostrate ourself before these idols is our wily
self-serving. To turn from these gods is to hear and respond to the call, "Repent!"

Believe

The point we turn to in conversion is the Light that
overcomes the darkness. *Epistrophe* is to that lumines-
cence as *metanoia* is to the night powers. Such a believing turning *to* comes on the heels of a repentant turning
from. It is a orientation to the God who has vanquished
the gods.

The event that triggers this turning is the sighting of the
dawn, the discovery of the good news that the life, death,
and resurrection of Jesus herald the demise of the powers
of darkness. Belief is that moment in conversion when the
one who turns "sees the light." To see the light is to take
our bearings from the dayspring rather than the nightfall,
to orient ourselves to the horizon rise of the Easter God
who is above every dark god, the name that is above
every name. This Light announces to the seer, "Night is
over. Day has come. Accept the fresh situation. Join the
new age. Know that you live and move and have your
being in this Light. You are 'in Christ,' in the Light. See it.
Walk in it. Believe!"

The inseparability of repentance from belief is apparent
in the anticipatory allusions in the previous section to the
good news that liberates and humbles. In fact, some belief
must precede repentance; we catch a glimpse of horizon
glow even before we turn from the darkness. Yet the full

20. Cf. Harvey Cox, *On Not Leaving It to the Snake* (New York:
Macmillan, 1967), pp. vii-xviii.

affirmation of that dawn reality comes only when we turn toward it.

The Pauline code word for such affirmation is "faith." Faith fixes on the problem of human perversity at the heart of our turning our backs on God and neighbor. Faith is our response to God's dealings with the powers of darkness that entice us. Their spell has been broken by the Easter sun. Faith is the eye lifted to that horizon.

Faith has been understood in the Christian tradition as both "assent" and "trust." Thus faith is an act of the head that hears with its ears the word that God in Christ is ready to accept us in spite of our submission to the blandishments of darkness. Mercy covers our guilt. But faith is also an act of the heart, one that throws itself in trust on this mercy and is buoyed up in profound and personal ways by its power. To believe in God is to have faith that the source of our wrongs has been dealt with, our beguilement is forgiven, our ruptures are healed, and a way back is possible, not by our merit, but by God's grace.

To believe is to hope as well as to assent and trust. Faith covers a sorry past. Hope, its partner, stretches toward a promising future. As faith deals with our sin and guilt, hope copes with our tempters and captors. To hope is to believe that the future, once controlled by the principalities and powers, has been opened. Hope is an appetite whetted for the not yet. The powers of darkness, whose sovereignty over our lives and our historical future seemed so secure, have met their match in Jesus Christ. Karl Barth's counsel to British Christians in the midst of World War II speaks to us as we face our own principalities and powers: "The world in which we live is the place where Jesus Christ rose from the dead. . . . It is on

this world in its entirety that God has set His mark. . . . He
has exalted the name of Jesus above every name, 'that in
the name of Jesus every knee should bow, of things in
heaven and things on earth and things under the earth'
(Phil. 2:10). Since this is true, the world in which we live
is not some sinister wilderness where fate or chance holds
sway or where all sorts of 'principalities and powers' run
riot unrestrained and range about unchecked. Since this
is true, the world has not been given up to the devil or to
man that they may make of it some vast 'Insanity
Fair.' . . . The Kingly rule of Christ extends not merely over
the Church as the congregation of the faithful but, regard-
less whether men believe it or not, over the whole of the
universe in all its heights and depths; and it also confronts
and overrules with sovereign dignity the principalities
and powers and evil spirits of this world. . . . For Jesus
Christ, according to the teaching of the whole New Testament, has already borne away sin and destroyed death.
So also has He already (Col. 2:15) completely disarmed
those 'principalities and powers' and made a spectacle of
them in His own triumph in order finally to tread them
down under His feet on the day of His coming again (I
Cor. 15:15). It is only as shadows without real substance
and power that they can still beset us. We Christians, of all
men, have no right whatsoever to fear and respect them or
to resign ourselves to the fact that they are spreading
throughout the world as though they knew neither
bounds nor lord. We should be slighting the resurrection
of Jesus Christ and denying His reign on the right hand of
the Father, if we forget that the world in which we live is
already consecrated, and if we did not, for Christ's sake,

come to grips spiritedly and resolutely with these evil spirits."[21]

Unbelief breeds despair, and despair immobilizes. But hope mobilizes. Belief, as the assurance of an open future, releases us for action toward it.

An Excursus on Foreshortened Journeys

On the pilgrimage of conversion, we must watch next for a fatal misstep. Too many interpretations and experiences of Christian turning end their journey with repentance and belief. To do so is to flirt with the interiorizing of conversion. This confusion would abort the new birth. The consciousness-transformation of repentance and belief does not exhaust the meaning of conversion. The disastrous pietism and privatism to which Christianity in our time has shown itself especially vulnerable is directly related to this misunderstanding. Lesslie Newbigin has gone to the heart of the matter: "The idea that one is first converted, and then looks around to see what one should do as a consequence, finds no basis in Scripture. . . . A careful study of the biblical use of the language of conversion, of returning to the Lord, will show that . . . it is always in the context of concrete decision at a given historical moment."[22]

Indeed, it is often acknowledged that subsequent to inner change of heart there will be outer reorientation.

21. Karl Barth, *A Letter to Great Britain from Switzerland* (London: Sheldon Press, 1941), pp. 9-11.

22. Lesslie Newbigin, *The Finality of Christ* (Richmond: John Knox, 1969), pp. 93f.

This claim not only fails to do justice to the biblical characterizations of conversion but it also ignores the empirical data. The latter have been summed up by black writer Louis Lomax, who remarks that whenever he drives into a "Bible belt" section of the country and hears on his car radio the shouting evangelists, he thinks to himself, "Look out Lomax, this is Klan country." Failure to understand that the threshold commitment must include turning to other human beings as well as to the divine other, love of neighbor as well as love of God, is the constant peril of pietist evangelism.

Thus the authenticity of conversion is marked by the presence in it of the ultimate goal of it. The end pre-exists in the means in conversion as in proclamation. This can be interpreted both normatively and descriptively. On the one hand, what eventuates is controlled by what initiates. And on the other, the outcome sought must be visible in the route toward it. If the ground and goal of conversion, the target of turning, is the God of shalom, who wills not only a new person, but a new community and a new earth, then the act of orienting oneself to that vision must manifest in itself those characteristics. To express this in our light imagery, as indicated in our telling of the story, Christian turning is not only seeing the Light, but seeing *by* the Light. And what we see in new light of that dawn is both the Christian community and the neighbor in need. That is why the full turn of conversion involves not only the move to repent and believe, but also the decision to be baptized and serve. These last turning points we now examine.

Be Baptized

Douglas Webster has observed that "there is a great

deal more in the New Testament about baptism than conversion."[23] Recent studies in New Testament conversion have helped to recover the baptismal theme obscured by heavy subjectivities. "So far as being antithetic to grace and faith, as much Protestant thought has in the past imagined, baptism is the sacrament of justification by faith. . . . They [the New Testament references to baptism] all make it abundantly clear that baptism and conversion belong together; it is the sacrament of once-for-all-ness, of incorporation into Christ."[24]

Baptism is one phase of conversion that marks the process as more than a change of heart and head. It is a change of location. It means new relationships and a new community. Conversion, as a threshold commitment to Christian faith, includes passage through the doorway of a new household. Baptism is that portal of entry. It is a turning toward and into that people who repent and believe.

Here our light metaphor helps to distinguish Christianity from alternative styles of spirituality. There are forms of religious perception which advise us to cling to the light we see, never to take our eyes off it, to contemplate it and meditate on it. The experience of seeing the light becomes the center of religion, and religious practice becomes the cultivation of light-mesmerism.

There is another way of relating to light. In the Christian story, seeing the light means, indeed, taking the horizon point as our fundamental reference. But it does not mean being hypnotized by it. Light is made to be seen by, not to

23. Webster, *op. cit.*, p. 165. For a fruitful discussion of the relation of the sacrament to conversion (interpreted as experience), see the discussion on pp. 163-80.

24. Green, *op. cit.*, pp. 152f.

be stared at. To use it, and see by it, represents a different life-style from fixation on it. Light in this tale is given to illumine the world so we can make our way in it. It is given most of all so that we can see other people. The range of this visible humanity is immense. For now, we speak about one segment, the brother and sister in Christ. Illumination brings the children of light together into the family of God, the church.

To the corporate is added the mobile. The posture appropriate to gazing is sitting, symbolized by the cross-legged position of the guru. Such a posture is consonant with a spirituality that seeks to transport the self out of this world. The position for those who use the light to see by is rather that of the pilgrim moving in the world. The turned sun-sighter is a dawn pilgrim. And in the act of baptism, the pilgrim affirms that the journey is not a solo trip but participation in a company of pilgrims. Dawn pilgrims are a dawn people.

This reaching out to the other is expressed by Paul as the third great Christian virtue. If faith and hope are response in belief to seeing the Light, then love is the patient, kind, and questing outreach to that community of believers made visible by the light. Baptism is the sign by which we affirm the communal character of the Christian tale, the seal of our love for other storytellers.[25]

25. For other dimensions of the sacrament of baptism, see Gabriel Fackre, "The Baptismal Encounter" (Lancaster Theological Seminary Occasional Paper No. 1, 1962), pp. 7-32. While John Baillie's study *Baptism and Conversion* (New York: Scribners, 1963) too closely identifies conversion with "conversion experience" it does succeed in holding together personal and communal, subjective and objective motifs; see pp. 104-12. I have also sought to deal with the relation of baptism to personal faith in *What Happens in Baptism?* (Philadelphia: Geneva Press, 1967). In churches that practice infant baptism, the conversion process does not unfold in a way comparable to the "missionary situation" of the first century or similar times and places. Baptism as an act of incorporation into the Christian community is prior to repentance, belief, and service. In terms of our light metaphor, the pilgrim parents and congregation bear the child in their arms on the journey in the baptismal event. The sleeping infant whose eyes do not see the light is, nevertheless, oriented toward the horizon by this support community. The

Serve

The act of love is by no means exhausted by life together in the family of God. It is care for the outcast and oppressed as well as the community of faith. It is seeing in the Light the unseen, the invisible of the earth. This love for the unloved is the decisive test of the authenticity of conversion. "By their fruits you shall know them."

The final phase of turning, therefore, is serving. Conversion begins in repentance and is climaxed by service: clothing the naked, feeding the hungry, visiting prisoners, doing justice, making peace. To understand servanthood as part and parcel of conversion is to bring it in at the threshold—rather than at some later point—in the Christian life. To position it only subsequent to conversion is a perennial and fatal temptation. Of course, good works do flow from the initial turning. But more fundamentally, the very act of conversion, of doing an about-face, *includes* bending down to offer the cup of cold water to those in need. The "fruits meet for repentance" (Matt. 3:8; Luke 3:8; Acts 26:20) are part of the original posture. And turning from the darkness is only validated as a turn to the light when we see by it, as well as orient ourselves toward it. "Whoever says that he is in the light, yet hates his brother, is in the darkness. . . . Whoever loves his brother stays in the light" (I John 2:9-10 TEV).

A full turn is the only one that puts us on the right road. Otherwise we wander off and lose the way. The "people of the Way," as the early Christians were called, are given through conversion a new vision that opens their eyes to the victims battered by the bandits on the Jericho Road.

---

conversion process unfolds as the maturing child, borne forward by others, opens its eyes to see the rays in which it is bathed, descends to walk on its own feet and take its place in the ranks of the seeing and serving company. In the infant baptism tradition, the rite of confirmation provides an occasion for the personal owning of the forward momentum.

Those who cannot see by the light pass by on the other side. Those who have truly turned see and serve.

A seeing service is not just "social service." World Council of Churches biblical studies in conversion move Paul Loffler to affirm, "There is an indissoluble relation between 'conversion' and 'social action.'[26] The one who sees Jericho Road victims deals with the bandits as well as after-effects of banditry. The powers of darkness roam the road. Evils inherent in the system imperil the traveler. Servanthood must contest the social, economic, and political structures which oppress. Road patrols that prevent the assaults mean just and human social designs, which assure bread for the hungry, freedom for the slave, power for the powerless, peace for the war-ravaged. Seeing the Light and seeing by it is the vision to see as well the encroachment of the dark principalities whose shadows are longest at the dawn.

Repent, believe, be baptized, serve—these are the movements that constitute conversion. With the help of our biblical words and images, we can identify this process as a re-positioning of the self, a turning away from darkness toward the Easter dawn, a turning to see the Light of the risen Son, and to see by it the company of pilgrims and the neighbor in need. Lesslie Newbigin captures this transaction in comparable imagery: "Conversion, then, means being turned around in order to recognize and participate in the dawning reality of God's reign. But this inward turning immediately and intrinsically involves both a pattern of conduct and a visible companionship. It involves a membership in a community and a decision to act in certain ways."[27]

26. Paul Loffler, "The Biblical Concept of Conversion," *Study Encounter,* I. No. 2 (1965), 94.

27. Newbigin, *op. cit.,* p. 32.

"I . . . Not I"

The further we probe conversion and see it as a choice that costs us something, the more we confront a familiar paradox of Christian teaching. The very movements that appear to be efforts of our will to repent, to believe, be baptized and serve, are in fact enabled by the grace of Another. Paul, reflecting on his own decisions, records a perennial Christian insight: "By God's grace I am what I am, nor has his grace been given to me in vain; on the contrary, in my labours I have outdone them all—not I, indeed, but the grace of God working with me" (I Cor. 15:10 NEB). Jonathan Edwards puts the same paradox in these terms: "In efficacious grace we are not merely passive, nor yet does God do *some* and we do the *rest*. But God does all, and we do all. God produces all, and we act all. For that is what he produces, viz. our own acts. God is the only proper author and founder; we are the proper actors."[28] In prospect the decision and effort of turning appears to be our own. This day we must choose. In retrospect we acknowledge that our repentance, faith, baptism, and service are made possible by the power of God working in, with, and under our powers. The turn we make is "the gift of conversion," as Erik Routley describes it in his fine essay on threshold commitment.

The divine initiative that evokes and empowers our turning, the warm sun on our backs and the lighted sky we glimpse out of the corner of our eye, is described in many

28. Jonathan Edwards, "Concerning Efficacious Grace," *The Works of President Edwards* (Leeds: Edward Baines, 1811), VIII, 454. See James Sellers' helpful comments on this subject in *Theological Ethics* (New York: Macmillan, 1966), pp. 39-53. Note also D.M. Baillie's discussion of the paradoxes of faith, *God Was in Christ,* pp. 106-13.

ways in Christian devotion and thought. Like the word "conversion" these images have not been comfortably used in mainstream Christianity. Our uneasiness with the terms has left a vacuum filled by others all too ready to appropriate biblical symbols for their own purposes. Those meanings dominate today. What do you think about when you hear the phrase "being born again"? Who speaks with fervor about "the baptism of the Holy Spirit"? Who asks, "Are you saved"? This great ancient language describing the power that makes possible our turning has been captured by narrow partisans. As a postscript to the dynamics of conversion, we point toward some soteriological words and themes that cry out for repossession by the whole faith community.

The New Birth

The figure of new birth is drawn from a universal human experience. It clearly identifies conversion as something done to us rather than by us. It leaves no doubt that it is a power not our own that brings a new creature into the light of the day. Again, it is a clear statement that conversion is a process, and a laborious one, which moves through those stages of gestation and deliverance we have sought to identify as repentance, belief, baptism, and service. Birth is a time of newness and radical change; it is, literally, a passage from darkness to light, a fit term for the total reorientation of conversion. Also, new birth marks conversion as a starting point, not the finish of the matter. Those who are converted are infants in the faith. There is much maturation yet to come. "Born again Christians" have to grow into the fulness of the stature of

Christ. Fixation on the trauma of birth, on the experience of conversion, is an immature piety. Christians mesmerized by the return to the womb of faith are still babes in Christ, ready for milk but not strong meat. Finally, the new birth in many New Testament texts is associated with strange and surprising visible, tangible things, for which an exclusively interiorized conception of conversion is not prepared. Thus baptism is called the washing of regeneration, and Christ speaks about being born again by water and the Holy Spirit (Titus 3:5; John 3:5). This is one more reminder of how humble, pedestrian, objective events associated with participation in the Christian community are integral to the birth of the new Christian life.

The Holy Spirit

In classical Christian teaching, the Holy Spirit is the third person of the Trinity, the ongoing activity of deity that moves and shakes and changes the world. It is no accident that symbols for Spirit are wind and fire. Where the Spirit is, things happen!

Luther's Small Catechism (Article III) describes the work of the Spirit as calling, gathering, enlightening, and sanctifying. These divine movements make their presence felt in the conversion turn. Indeed, a case could be made for rough correspondence (repentance and calling, belief and enlightening, baptism and gathering, service and sanctifying). Of course, the Spirit is not limited to the individual stirrings with which we deal in conversion. The Holy Spirit ranges over the whole heights and depths of creation and history.[29] But "being born again by the Holy Spirit" is an essential work of the God who turns.

Salvation

What of the relation of salvation to conversion? Here we call again upon the light imagery to illuminate that much used and abused query, "Are you saved?"

When the dawn broke on Easter morning, the world *was* saved from the powers of darkness. We have all been liberated from this bondage. No more can the principalities of evil control the future.

What has taken place ontologically has not yet been fulfilled existentially. It is dawn, not high noon. The time in which we live is one in which the shadows still stretch across the land, a time of waiting for the fulfilment of the divine glory when "God is all in all." At this dawn is signaled the meridian which is to be, that luminous City of God: "By its light shall the nations walk, and the kings of the earth shall bring into it all their splendor. The gates of the city shall never be shut by day—and there will be no night!" (Rev. 21:24 NEB). Salvation is eschatological as well as historical. The world which has been saved in principle *will be* saved in fact. And it waits with eager longing and much groaning for that midday when nature, humanity, and deity shall dwell in shalom.

The salvation which was and will be is completed by the salvation which *is*. "Salvation Today" is the present

---

29. For attention to this larger landscape of the Spirit, see Wolfhart Pannenberg, "The Doctrine of the Spirit and the Task of the Theology of Nature," in Martin Marty and Dean Peerman (eds.), *New Theology No. 10* (New York: Macmillan, 1973), pp. 17-37; and Hendrikus Berkhof, *The Doctrine of the Holy Spirit* (Richmond: John Knox, 1964).

working of that future which breaks in on us. As recent World Council of Churches studies have stressed, this present soteriological current runs through all the movements of shalom in our history.[30] Where there is liberation and reconciliation in the political, economic, and social ferment, there is the incognito Christ with his saving grace. Yet the "right now" activity of shalom is not exhausted by the presences of the Kingdom in the larger theater of history. The eschatological and historical reach out for companionship with the personal. For those who have made the turn there is individual friendship with the Light. Being saved is knowing participation in and commitment to that healing process which was, is, and is to be. It is the taste of an *aperitif* of the heavenly banquet. It is partial and ambiguous, but no less real. As process and not product, it is not the simplistic "saved," but "being saved" from the powers of darkness that daily imperil us on our pilgrimage. It is walking in the Light.

Being saved is showing signs of the future that God wills for the world. That ultimate dream and promise of God is for a free and peaceable Kingdom of light. The evidence of that Kingdom's breakthrough in the life of a person is the presence of shalom. Wherever one is being grafted right now into the process set loose in the world by God in Jesus Christ, saving manifests itself in healing and the signs of freedom and peace in that life. Is there liberation and reconciliation manifest in this turned one? Is the Holy Spirit, the portent of the new age, manifest through visible fruits of the new age? Here we come full circle, returning to those acts which constitute conversion. The

30. See the *International Review of Mission* issue, "Meeting in Bangkok," LXII, No. 246 (Apr. 1973), 133-230.

clue to the Spirit's presence, the eschatological gifts, the evidence of the new birth, the signs of salvation are repentance, belief, baptism, and service. For in the Kingdom of shalom there will be no powers of darkness, no lethal egocentricity, but instead liberation from tyranny, a loving life together and a spontaneous overflowing of care for the other. Thus the light we reflect is a dim prefiguration of the day that shall be.

Temptation

Those mirrors we bear of the ultimate daylight are at best cracked and crusted reflectors. There is, in fact, a peculiar pattern to our distortions. Those who have caught something of the light tend to fix on one or another of the phases of conversion, absolutizing it and dispensing with the rest. We are prone to be satisfied with quarter turns and to march off on a tangent. The wrenching moment of turning—repentance—produces penitents who dwell remorselessly on the pains and joys of tearing loose. These are the pietists. Others have fixed on belief as the be-all and end-all of the Christian life, interpreting conversion as the rigid acceptance of doctrine. These are the dogmatists. There are also those turners who discover the community aspect of conversion (a life together that may run from the intense group experience to the routines of ecclesiastical existence), and absolutize it. These might be called the groupists. Finally, there are those who find their conversion identity in the doing and serving dimension, and have eyes for nothing else. These are the activists. Pietism, dogmatism, groupism, activism—each treats the part as a whole and in so doing shreds the whole cloth of conversion.

Pilgrimage

There is more to the Christian life than conversion. It is not enough to turn. We have to move. The Christian life is a new pilgrimage as well as a new posture.

That pilgrimage consists of the reenactment along the way of the commitments made at the outset of the journey. Each aspect of turning is relived as a step along the way. Luther asks us to remember our baptism each morning. We must go further and recall as well our initiatory repentance, our belief, and our service. The quarter turn of repentance emerges anew on pilgrimage as daily penitence for our continuing perversity and a daily contest with the powers that seek to enslave us. The turn of belief is reborn as the struggle to repossess our faith and hope. Each day we graft ourselves anew into the body of the baptized. Each morning we reposition ourselves on the Jericho Roads around us. In these rememberings, as at our initiation, we are buoyed by a strength not our own. The light is still on the horizon, even as we live in the grey dawn of continued struggle with our shadowside. The children of light are also the children of darkness. We have not arrived; we are pilgrims.

And pointers. That is evangelism, pointing—not up and out of this world but ahead, *through* this world to its horizon, to the God who beckons humanity to turn from darkness to Light, and in that Light to see the brother and sister in Christ and serve the neighbor in need.

Selected Bibliography

I. Books

Andersen, Wilhelm. *Towards a Theology of Mission*. London: SCM, 1955.

Anderson, Gerald (ed.). *The Theology of Christian Mission*. Nashville: Abingdon, 1961.

Baillie, John. *Baptism and Conversion*. New York: Scribners, 1963.

Barclay, William. *Turning to God: A Study of Conversion in the Book of Acts and Today*. Philadelphia: Westminster, 1964; Grand Rapids: Baker, 1973 (paperback reprint).

Boberg, John, and James Scherer (eds.). *Mission in the 1970s: What Direction?* Chicago Cluster of Theological Schools, 1972.

Brown, Fred. *Secular Evangelism*. London: SCM, 1970.

Christians, Clifford, Earl Schipper and Wesley Smedes. *Who in the World?* Grand Rapids: Eerdmans, 1972.

Costas, Orlando E. *The Church and Its Mission: A Shattering Critique from the Third World*. Wheaton: Tyndale, 1974.

Fackre, Gabriel. *Do and Tell: Engagement Evangelism in the '70s*. Grand Rapids: Eerdmans, 1973.

Fisher, Wallace. *Because We Have Good News*. Nashville: Abingdon, 1974.

Green, Michael. *Evangelism in the Early Church*. Grand Rapids: Eerdmans, 1970.

Hart, Julian. *Toward a Theology of Evangelism*. Nashville: Abingdon, 1955.

Hoekendijk, J.C. *The Church Inside Out.* Philadelphia: Westminster, 1966.

_____. *Horizons of Hope.* Nashville: Tidings, 1970.

Hunter, George (ed.). *Rethinking Evangelism.* Nashville: Tidings, 1971.

Jones, E. Stanley. *Conversion.* Nashville: Abingdon, 1959.

Kantonen, T.A. *Theology of Evangelism.* Philadelphia: Muhlenberg, 1954.

Krass, Alfred. *Beyond the Either-Or Church.* Nashville: Tidings, 1973.

Margull, Hans. *Hope in Action.* Translated by Eugene Peters. Philadelphia: Muhlenberg, 1962.

Maury, Philippe. *Politics and Evangelism.* New York: Doubleday, 1959.

McGavran, Donald (ed.). *The Eye of the Storm.* Waco, Tex.: Word, 1972.

_____. *Understanding Church Growth.* Grand Rapids: Eerdmans, 1969.

Moberg, David. *The Great Reversal: Evangelism Versus Social Concern.* Philadelphia: Lippincott, 1972.

Mouw, Richard J. *Political Evangelism.* Grand Rapids: Eerdmans, 1974.

Newbigin, Lesslie. *The Finality of Christ.* Richmond: John Knox, 1969.

Niles, D.T. *That They May Have Life.* London: Lutterworth, 1952.

Outler, Albert. *Evangelism in the Wesleyan Spirit.* Nashville: Tidings, 1972

Powers, Edward. *Signs of Shalom.* Philadelphia: United Church Press, 1973.

Poulton, John. *A Today Sort of Evangelism.* London: Lutterworth, 1972.

Routley, Erik. *The Gift of Conversion.* Philadelphia: Muhlenberg, 1960.

Sovik, Arne. *Salvation Today.* Minneapolis: Augsburg, 1973.

Stowe, David. *Ecumenicity and Evangelism.* Grand Rapids: Eerdmans, 1970.

Thomas, M.M. *Salvation and Humanisation.* Bangalore: Christian Institute for the Study of Religion and Society, 1971.

Tippett, Alan. *Church Growth and the Word of God.* Grand Rapids: Eerdmans, 1970.

Verkuyl, Johannes. *The Message of Liberation in Our Age.* Translated by Dale Cooper. Grand Rapids: Eerdmans, 1972.

Webster, Douglas. *What Is Evangelism?* London: The Highway Press, 1964.

Williams, Colin. *Where in the World?* New York: National Council of Churches, 1963.

Winter, Ralph (comp.). *The Evangelical Response to Bangkok.* Pasadena, Calif.: Wm. Carey Library, 1973.

II. Periodical and Journal Articles and Issues

"Evangelism Handbook." *A.D.,* III, No. 11 (Nov. 1974).

"Evangelism." *Andover Newton Quarterly*, XIV, No. 3 (Jan. 1974).

"Evangelism." *Dialog*, XII, No. 1 (Winter 1973).

"Evangelism: More of What?" *The Christian Ministry*, IV, No. 2 (March 1973).

"Humanisation and Mission." *International Review of Mission*, LX, No. 237 (Jan. 1971).

"Key '73." *Foundations*, XVI, No. 2 (Apr.-June 1973).

"Key '73: The New Evangelism?" *Christianity and Crisis*, XXXIII, No. 4 (March 19, 1973).

Mead, Loren. "Evangelism: Notes Toward a Better Understanding." *Anglican Theological Review*, LIII, No. 1 (Jan. 1971), 48-56.

Neill, Stephen. "Conversion." *Scottish Journal of Theology*, III, No. 4 (Dec. 1950), 352-62.

Newbigin, Lesslie. "Salvation and Humanisation." *Religion and Society*, XVIII, No. 1 (March 1971), 71-80.

"Perspectives on Evangelism." *JSAC Grapevine*, V, No. 2 (July 1973).

"Salvation Today II." *International Review of Mission*, LXI, No. 241 (Jan. 1972).

"Secularization and Conversion." *Study Encounter*, I, No. 2 (1965).

III. Church Resources and Reports

Bangkok Assembly 1973: Minutes and Report. Commission on World Mission and Evangelism, World Council of Churches, 1973.

Biblical Perspectives on Salvation. Commission on World Mission and Evangelism, World Council of Churches, 1972.

The Church for Others. Working Groups on the Missionary Structure of the Congregation, World Council of Churches, 1967.

Evangelism for a New Day. New York: United Church Board for Homeland Ministries, 1972.

"Evangelism: The Mission to Those Outside Her Life." Report of Section II, *Evanston Speaks*, pp. 18-25, World Council of Churches, 1954.

Evangelism Training Manual. New Materials Task Force, United Church Board for Homeland Ministries, 1974 (mimeograph).

"The Evangelization of the Modern World," *Crux Special* (August 3, 1973).

"New Life Mission Manual." Nashville: Tidings, 1974.

"Renewal and Mission." *The Uppsala Report*, pp. 21ff., World Council of Churches, 1968.

"Report of the Section on Witness." *New Delhi Speaks*, pp. 26-51, World Council of Churches, 1962.

Resources for Developing an Evangelistic Life Style. Valley Forge, Penna.: American Baptist Churches, 1972.

Salvation Today and Contemporary Experience. World Council of Churches, 1972.

"A Theological Reflection on the Work of Evangelism." *Bulletin,* V, No. 1-2 (Nov. 1959). Division of Studies, World Council of Churches.

The Thesis and Practice of Evangelism. Glasgow: The Iona Community House, 1947.

Toward a Working Definition of Evangelism. United Church Board for World Ministries, 1971.